Pe... Mastery

By Tyson Kilbey

Top Firearms Instruction

Copyright © 2020 by Tyson Kilbey

All rights reserved.

Cover design by Wayne Cooley

Book design by Wayne Cooley

No part of this book may be reproduced in any form or by any electronic or mechanical means including information storage and retrieval systems, without permission in writing from the author. The only exception is by a reviewer, who may quote short excerpts in a review.

Tyson Kilbey

Visit my website at
http://www.topfirearmsinstruction.com/

Printed in the United States of America

Table of Contents

Acknowledgements	4
Introduction	6
Foreword	13
Chapter 1 - Self-Defense Mindset	21
Chapter 2 - Defensive Driving	41
Chapter 3 - Empty Hand Self-Defense	65
Chapter 4 - Defensive Tools	82
Chapter 5 - Firearms	95
Chapter 6 - Personal Defense Extras	116
Chapter 7 - Training	135
Conclusion	156
Afterword	159
About the Author	164

Acknowledgements

One of the most reprehensible statistics I have ever heard is that one in four women will be assaulted at some point in their lives. I have heard other estimates which indicate that number may be as high as one out of every three women. Similarly, I have read statistics in which one in six men are assaulted at some point in their lives. These are *reported* statistics. This leads me to believe that these numbers are mere reference points and the actual numbers are indeed much higher.

A genuine feeling of safety and security for you and your family is not something that should be taken away from you. Unfortunately, there are evil people in the world who are willing to attack, injure, sexually assault, and ultimately murder innocent people. This book is for all of you who are willing to step up to the plate and stop that from happening in every way you are capable of. Even though I hope you never have to, I want you to have every advantage and preparation strategy in place in case you are called upon to act. At any moment in time, you could be the one and only thing that stops a tragedy from occurring. You are who this book is meant for.

To all of the people I acknowledged in *Fundamental Handgun Mastery*, I am still thankful for all that you do. My family, friends, training partners, and students past, present, and future: thank you. I hope to train with you soon!

Introduction

Self-defense is not just a set of techniques; it's a state of mind, and it begins with the belief that you are worth defending. –Rorion Gracie

In April 2018, I officially released my first book, *Fundamental Handgun Mastery.* In the Introduction section, I described the process of writing a book as a "challenging undertaking." To be clear, my feelings on the matter have not changed. Writing a book is time-intensive, and at times physically and mentally exhausting. I have also discovered that during the process you run the gamut of emotions; from confidence, elation, and also to moments of self-doubt. But most of all, writing a book gives the author a feeling of accomplishment that is virtually impossible to describe.

When I began reading the reviews of *Fundamental Handgun Mastery* shortly after it was published, I knew I had connected with many of the readers in a meaningful and powerful way. Furthermore, I accomplished my goal of reaching an audience that did not just include firearms enthusiasts. On the same day I received a message from a United States Practical Shooting

Association (USPSA) Grandmaster class shooter explaining how he picked up some philosophical concepts from the book, I received a message from a lady who was completely new to firearms. She explained that she immediately developed an appreciation for firearms safety, and the description of the fundamentals was something she was able to understand without prior experience or training. It was an exceptionally satisfying feeling to know the work I put into the book served to connect with people from such a wide variety of backgrounds and levels of experience. For years I have been teaching (and learning from) students who also represent a diverse background, so producing a book with that vision in mind was critically important.

Fundamental Handgun Mastery was a culmination of nearly eighteen years of law enforcement experience, countless competitive shootings events, firearms instructor courses throughout the country, training with some of the most accomplished shooters in the industry, and training thousands of law enforcement officers and civilians in a variety of classes.

I am extremely thrilled and satisfied by who the book has reached, and what it has accomplished. But I knew almost immediately that I wasn't done. I have devoted nearly my entire life to the study of martial arts and self-defense, and a substantial portion of my adult life to teaching self-defense and firearms. Firearms use and training is only one element of self-defense. I often remind myself and my students of the saying, "When your only tool is a hammer, then every problem becomes a nail." Personal defense is a lifelong endeavor that encompasses many components. Because threats to safety are as numerous and varied as they are, a layered and scalable approach is the most effective strategy to meet the demand. To that end, I would not be giving everything I have learned over a lifetime of study the correct energy and emphasis it deserves by only writing a book about firearms. This book is not about fear, but preparation, confidence, and empowerment in all areas of life. So, welcome to *Personal Defense Mastery*.

This book comes with the culmination of now twenty years of law enforcement experience and hundreds of additional hours of self-defense and firearms-related training events. In this book, I will explore self-defense from several different perspectives and angles. In virtually every one of my classes, regardless of the topic of focus, I explain to my students the previously mentioned concept that true self-defense involves a layered, multi-faceted approach. Anyone who believes that by training with a handgun exclusively, they are preparing themselves for personal defense is quite honestly deceiving themselves. For example, if someone practices with their handgun, but does not know any empty-hand self-defense techniques, doesn't take care of themselves physically or mentally, doesn't drive safely, and doesn't understand how to effectively communicate and de-escalate potentially volatile situations, then are they truly invested in self-defense?

In *Personal Defense Mastery* we will explore self-defense from a variety of angles. I intend that at some point, in some chapter, I will help the reader discover some facet of personal safety they may have not previously thought about. But beyond that, I am going to share my proven roadmap to not only address and prepare for these self-defense scenarios, but also how I have managed to enjoy every minute of it along the way. The value that will bring is this: when we as humans enjoy something, we tend to share it with others. This is one of the secrets I have discovered along the way. Imagine the impact of sharing something with someone that one day may be the very thing that saves their life. That is an exciting and worthwhile endeavor that deserves to be explored!

In my last book, I explained the amazing opportunities I have had to train alongside some of the best shooters, fighters, and most knowledgeable law enforcement officers in the world. As incredible as those experiences have been, it is equally if not more enjoyable and fulfilling to train with people for the very first time. To see the spark and amazement in a beginner's eyes when they correctly perform their first Jiu-Jitsu technique is an experience that never gets old. When I see a nervous yet anxious student successfully fire a gun and observe the placement of the shot on their target, for a brief moment, the shared experience brings me back to learning that skill for the first time. Most teachers I have spoken with understand this almost magical feeling.

Whether you are a young man or woman who is preparing to go off to college and want to learn more about personal protection, or a middle-aged mother or father with a family who would like to invest time and energy into learning how to make your family safer, or a victim of domestic abuse, bullying, or any and everything in between, there is something in this book for you. Our unique life experiences are part of us, but in no way do they have to define us. In this book I will discuss the pros and cons of a variety of self-defense tools, I will examine empty-hand martial arts, I will dedicate a chapter exclusively to firearms and yet another to the importance of safe driving. Never will I say that the ways, systems, styles, and perspectives that I have chosen are the only correct way. Instead, I will share with you my mindset and the process by which I have made my decisions. I will share with you stories from students, personal experiences, articles that I have written for various magazines that reinforce the principles of this book, and some of the Training Tips of the Day that I have shared in blogs and social media pages for my company Top Firearms Instruction. I expect that in some areas we will agree, and in other aspects of self-defense, we will not. That is part of what makes the topic of personal safety so fascinating. There are many unique ways to accomplish the objective.

Thank you for joining me for this experience and I hope this book will educate and inspire you to be safer and more prepared in an ever-changing world. Whether you have read *Fundamental Handgun Mastery* and this is our second journey together, or this is the first time we have explored these topics together; I hope that not only you, but your friends, family, and loved ones will join you in your quest to become safer and more prepared to meet the challenges of personal safety.

For those of you thinking, this all sounds great, but there is no way in the world that I have time to train in all of the many areas of personal defense, do not worry! "Not having the time" is the number one excuse that humans make to not accomplish something, even when they concede it is worth doing. It is not the time that is the problem, every single day has the same amount of hours in it, and it is the same for all of us. It is a question of prioritization and efficiency when using that time. So in this book, I will share with you several ways that these different skills connect and overlap, and how you can maximize your results in the fastest amount of time possible. But more importantly, I do not doubt that when you identify these common themes you will discover your own unique ways to train and prepare for yourself.

To end this introduction and welcome to *Personal Defense Mastery,* I want to share with you the powerful mindset that one of my self-defense instructors shared with me, and I have in turn shared with many of my students: "Self-defense is not just a set of techniques; it's a state of mind, and it begins with the belief that you are worth defending." Once you realize that truth, it is important to take it one step further. Because you are worth defending, take ownership and responsibility over that fact and make yourself the most difficult target a potential attacker would ever want to threaten. Enjoy the book friends and let's get started.

Foreword

Growing up, I loved movies like *The Incredibles* and *Avengers*. I loved the idea of there being superheroes to save the world.

In 2015, a story hit the news that forever changed my perception of superheroes. A train filled with passengers was headed from Amsterdam to Paris. A man began to open fire with an AK47. Anthony Sadler, Alek Skarlatos, and Spencer Stone tackled the gunman. Using his jiu-jitsu skills, Spencer Stone choked the attacker unconscious before anyone was killed. At the time, I had no idea what jiu-jitsu was, but the idea that there were real life superheroes out there who could stop the violence was forever embedded in my memory.

Flash forward to 2017, I was in the college atmosphere and working in law enforcement. I had friends who had been sexually assaulted, and realized I was an easy target being a small female. I had a close experience one night when two men came banging on my door at 11pm.

"I know she's there," one of them said. "I saw her go in there over an hour ago." Knowing maintenance never came past 8pm, and not knowing who else it might be, I called 911 when they began kicking the door. When the officer arrived, the men identified themselves as maintenance and claimed they "just had the wrong door." Soon after, I came home to find a cigarette lighter on my living room floor, with no notification from the apartment complex. I began to feel very unsafe in my own home and started looking for ways to defend myself. When a coworker told me that Tyson taught jiu-jitsu, I was determined to try it, despite the fact I had never trained martial arts or been in a fight outside of scenario training.

One of the first things Tyson said to me was, "there are no bad students, only bad teachers." Tyson was the complete opposite of a bad instructor. By the end of that first class he had taught me the 'trap and roll,' a jiu-jitsu technique that uses leverage to overcome a stronger opponent. I quickly realized that superheroes were no longer confined to movies or stories in the news. I had met a superhero who not only possessed the skills of self-defense, but was willing to teach me as well. As of now, I have trained with Tyson for over three years. He has been my mentor and instructor in firearms training and jiu-jitsu through my blue belt, in addition to helping me certify as a women's self-defense instructor.

Like all superhero stories, there are enormous odds to face. Terrorist attacks, shootings, human trafficking… the list goes on and on. However, as Tyson has told me before, "You can't control the situation, but you can control your response to it." We can't control the terrible events that happen, but how we respond can change everything. It is the ordinary people who train and are mentally prepared who become the Spencer Stone in a crisis. You will be in situations that no one else will, and when violence occurs, will you be ready?

Readers of Tyson's first book, *Fundamental Handgun Mastery*, know what a gem it is. There was so much I took away from it, especially as a novice in firearms. *Personal Defense Mastery* went above and beyond my expectations. It's rare to find a self-defense book that is compelling as well as practical. Tyson covers everything from mindset, verbal de-escalation, martial arts, handgun proficiency, safe driving, and active shooter situations, to name a few. My favorite part about this book is the 'Most Important Concepts' at the end of each chapter. These are easy to refer back to, and are great tools to practice with.

This is the time to take personal self-defense in your own hands. No one is born jiu-jitsu choking people or having the perfect aim in a shooting competition. But with some training and this book as a guide, you too can become that superhero.

-Elizabeth Henderson

****

*****

Dear Reader,

I've known the author, Tyson Kilbey, for several years now. He is a respected colleague and a good friend. If you've read his first book, Fundamental Handgun Mastery, you undoubtedly already know how we met at one of his first Kids Handgun Safety courses. Since that time, I have continued my advocacy with 1 Million Moms Against Gun Control (1MMAGC), and have since partnered with The DC Project, founded by Diana Muller, as well as co-hosting the podcast To The Republic, with Timothy Knight.

Throughout this time I have continued to earnestly follow Tyson's career in self-defense instruction. I have attend courses as my schedule allows and have unceasingly encouraged others to seek training from him and his associates at Top Firearms Instruction. After all, even after working with instructors across the nation, those I met so many years ago just outside of my hometown, are some of the best I've had the opportunity to work with and their courses come with my most sincere recommendation.

In picking up this book you are about to embark on a glimpse into a collection of self-defense techniques which stem from a cumulative 20 years of law enforcement, personal pursuits of hands-on education from the best-of-the-best self-defense instructors, and a decade of meeting students where they are, at their personal level of mental and physical preparedness, and working alongside of them to teach individualized techniques in order to reach, and often exceed, their personal defense goals.

Throughout these chapters, you will glean valuable information such as situational awareness, de-escalation, non-weapon and weapon defense, defensive driving, and so much more.

One of my favorite things about Tyson's methodology when it comes to self-defense training is that he acknowledges that what might work in one situation may not be the best choice in another. He is adamant about teaching his students a myriad of tools and techniques which they can have instantaneously available at their disposal on a moment's notice. Because, quite frankly, that's exactly how much time you have in an emergency self-defense situation.

It is my great pleasure to continue to learn from Tyson, whether I am attending a Top Firearms Instruction course, reading his books, interviewing him for a podcast episode, or simply having a conversation over a green smoothie (his choice, not mine). However, as much as I have enjoyed my years of learning from him, I am far more excited to be sharing his real-life application of self-defense with you. Your life is worth defending; and since it is worth defending, it is worth defending to the very best of your ability. I know that this book is merely a single step in your journey to learning about self-defense, but as far as first steps go, I can assure you in all confidence that you are on the right path.

Rebecca Schmoe

Chapter 1 - Self-Defense Mindset

Your mindset is your primary weapon –Jeff Cooper

The human mind is our fundamental resource. – John F. Kennedy

During the last ten years teaching both civilians and law enforcement officers in a variety of self-defense and personal safety courses, one of the most fascinating aspects of the training has been the mental game. Everything from developing the mental edge, using your mind to develop the awareness necessary for survival, performing mental rehearsals, critically reviewing situations and incidents that have occurred to discover the lessons learned, staying motivated to train and prepared to defend yourself in a multitude of different capacities, and developing the image which portrays that you are not an easy target. At the heart of the matter, I have come to truly believe this: Any and every great physical achievement and success started as a manifestation of the brilliant human mind. This is precisely why I have chosen to dedicate the first chapter to mindset.

It is amazing the amount of value that comes from discussing the philosophical aspects of self-defense, particularly after a training session. It is also incredible to hear stories that people have to share from their personal experiences. By no means do I require that of my students, but despite that, so many have willingly recounted situations they have been in, how they felt as a result, and what they learned from it. Throughout the years, students have described (oftentimes in great detail) physical attacks, robberies, shootings, home invasions, and sexual assaults. Very few things are more powerful than a survivor of a violent crime or personal attack openly sharing their thoughts, feelings, and lessons learned from the event. At this time, every training session I conduct, whether it is in a personal or a group setting, has some element of a mental and philosophical reflection. I believe this a critical, but often overlooked, portion of training.

In this chapter, I will discuss some of what I have discovered in regard to the mental aspect of self-defense. First, the recognition and understanding of how powerful the human mind is in terms of self-defense. Countless times through the years I have heard instructors say that the mind is the most powerful tool we humans carry. I do not disagree. Furthermore, I will discuss awareness principles that are essential to developing a self-defense mindset. Finally, I will detail the power of perspective and attitude.

Developing the mental edge in any endeavor is important, but it can be critical to survival, especially in worse case scenarios. Two things have worked best for me in developing this mental edge. First, is what many refer to as tactical or combat breathing. Whether I am managing the stress of a shooting or grappling competition, or an emergency call for service, slow, deliberate, long breaths in which you deeply inhale and then exhale completely has proven to be extremely helpful. There are many styles and techniques for breathing, but there is virtually universal agreement that one of the primary secrets to developing the mental edge in any arena of life is to manage and control your breathing. I recommend beginning to utilize deep, controlled, breathing immediately. I started by only using focused breathing techniques for a few minutes a day. Now, I use the power of breathing techniques multiple times a day and in virtually every stressful situation I encounter. On essentially every survey conducted of problems and challenges people face in the world, stress is in some form or another extremely high on the list. I would suggest deep, slow breathing is the number one thing you can do immediately to not only increase your focus and relax your mind but also successfully handle any problem you encounter.

The second tip I have used to develop the mental edge is consciously striving to be present in the moment. At the time of this writing, this is an area that a significant number of people can benefit from. In a fast-paced world constantly riddled with the temptation of distraction, it is entirely possible to go through an entire day or week of activities without ever really being "present" in the moment. When I have applied this concept to training, almost immediately my training sessions (regardless of the topic) have become more productive and meaningful. Beginning right now, make a conscious effort to be more present in each moment. Once you do, and you see the other ninety-five percent of the world around you engrossed in their cell phones, everything will begin to change for you. Notice the environment around you and focus on nothing but your feelings and observations at the present moment. Couple this process with tactical breathing, and there is zero doubt that you will begin to develop the mental edge. Furthermore, your presence in the moment will be clear to any potential attackers. You automatically become a less desirable target with increased "in the moment" awareness. Everyone I know can benefit mentally from these two tips. For most people reading this, if you apply these concepts, the results will be game-changing.

As a self-defense instructor, one of the most powerful training tools I not only use but teach my students is the process of mental rehearsal. I wrote about this in *Fundamental Handgun Mastery* and for good reason. It works. Successful athletes have been using positive mental rehearsal for years. There is absolutely no reason we should not be using this tool to make ourselves safer, more prepared, and more confident to deal with personal defense situations. The process is simple. Before or after training sessions, or during periods of free time, visualize scenarios you may find yourself in. It could be as simple as a verbal disagreement to a serious event such as an active shooter situation. Visualize yourself successfully diffusing or handling the incident. When you visualize your scenarios, attempt to see as much detail as you possibly can for maximum benefit. I believe this powerful concept builds confidence by actually programming your mind for success. Mental rehearsal is the positive counterpart of self-doubt and negative self-talk. Begin by doing this at least once a day even for only a few minutes. When you become skilled at mental rehearsal, you start to do it before all types of potentially stressful or unnerving activities. In the world of law enforcement, this critical strategy has been passed down by quality training officers to newer officers many times over. This practice is sometimes

referred to as asking yourself the "What if's?".
When an officer is on patrol driving through their
district between calls, many of them are running
potential scenarios through their mind to more
safely and effectively deal with high-stress
encounters and emergency calls for service. For
me, mental rehearsal has been an enormously
beneficial tool in more situations than I can count.

Another powerful tool for personal safety
is critical mental review. For law enforcement
officers, this is fairly simple because so many of
their activities are captured on camera. Reviewing
these videos allows officers to analyze their
tactics, positioning, and any other number of
factors to formulate an honest assessment
regarding how a situation was handled. But there
is no reason why all of us cannot review situations
we have been in and analyze what we did well,
and what we can do to improve. Furthermore, we
can view incidents that others have been involved
in to discover what lessons can be learned. Some
people look down on this process and describe it
as "Monday morning quarterbacking." But the
reality is there is a substantial difference between
criticizing the actions of others with the benefit of
hindsight, and taking a constructive look at a self-
defense situation and attempting to discover ways
to more effectively respond to similar incidents in
the future.

The next aspect of mental self-defense I want to share is how to stay motivated to train. Whether you spend time training at a martial arts academy, a fitness center or gym, or the firing range, it is inevitable that you will experience the highs, the lows, and the plateaus that come with the consistent training that is necessary to become proficient enough to defend yourself. Many people fall victim to this reality, and even though they know that consistent, focused practice is by far the best way to prepare, they often end up not training very often or even stop training altogether.

How I have faced this challenge through the years is a three-pronged approach. First, training MUST be an enjoyable experience. I know many instructors disagree with me on this one. Several instructors claim that training must be tough, laborious, and painful to be truly effective. I do not disagree that some training sessions should be structured in such a way that you push yourself to sometimes painful limits to get out of your comfort zone and grow from the experience. But, I disagree that most or even half of training sessions need to be this way. The development of skill takes time. For me, the only way to ensure that I will be at the range, the mat room, or the gym consistently is to design training sessions that are fun. This might not work for everyone, but for me, it is that simple.

My second strategy to stay motivated is the belief in the adage that your number one competition is you. I know this is cliché but I am more convinced than ever that it is completely true. It is one of the best perspectives you can have when training. Do not get me wrong, it can be both fun and a source of motivation to compete against other people. But ultimately the biggest and most important gauge for all of your progress is how you are developing in relation to your previous self. Once you realize this and truly believe it, you will start to see the progress you make.

My third and final prong in my motivation strategy will probably surprise you. When I do not feel like training, I skip it. I know this contrary to what so many people say in terms of sticking with it. It is a common belief that you should force yourself to train even on the days you do not want to. Many people believe that you have to do this because if you do not you will fall out of the pattern of training and quit. But my question is, how many people who subscribe to this mentality quit anyway? I have been training since I was 5 years old and to this day consistently train several times a week. My philosophy behind this approach is that when I constantly have to push myself to train even when I do not want to, training becomes a burden or a chore. Eventually, it will become something that I completely dread and will quit like so many people do. But, if I take days off when I do not feel like training, I am usually more excited and motivated to return to the mat or the range. Training becomes a choice and not an obligation when you apply this perspective. I know this is contrary to popular opinion, but this approach has worked incredibly well for me. I am willing to bet most of you have not heard this and have been forcing yourself to do the opposite. Try the strategy that I am suggesting here and see what it does for you. You're welcome.

The next concept I want to address in terms of mindset is the importance of awareness, listening to your instincts, resisting the urge to rationalize signs of danger, and developing important practices that will decrease your chance of being the target of an attack.

Almost every safety and self-defense related course available will at some point address the importance of awareness. The reason this is the case is that your level of awareness of your environment around you is directly related to how prepared you are to deal with a personal attack. The more you scan the area for danger the more you see, and the less opportunity you have to be taken by surprise. Which incidentally, is exactly what an attacker wants. So by being more present in the moment as I addressed earlier in the chapter, and more aware of your surroundings, the less likely you are to be the target of an attack. Even if you are the target of an attack, an increased awareness level will give you the best opportunity to formulate a plan to defend yourself.

I often get asked what you should be looking for when you are scanning the environment around you. The answer almost always depends on where you are and in what context. But the general principles are; escape routes from danger and avenues in which you could be approached, objects or other items that could be used as improvised weapons if the need were to arise, people who appear to be acting strangely or who appear to be observing you unusually, and any barriers that you could run to in order to buy time and put space between you and an attacker. These are the basics, and as you practice this level of awareness it gets easier and begins to happen more naturally. If you do it enough, you will get to the point that you barely have to consciously think about it. It just becomes part of how you see your environment. Sometimes students will ask if they do this, "Won't I just become overly paranoid and constantly be in a state of fear and hypervigilance?" Although that is a fair question, the answer is that it is entirely possible to be aware of your environment and ready to act if necessary, without being in a constant state of anxiety and paranoia. Furthermore, the level at which you are employing your situational awareness is always scalable to the time of day, location, and any other potential vulnerabilities you may have in your defenses. I can break this concept down to its simplest form by saying this: If something or someone does not seem right, do not ignore your instincts. Whatever is making you feel that way probably deserves your attention.

Now that we have discussed awareness of your environment, I want to discuss specific behaviors to notice about people. To truly be mentally focused, prepared, and aware, it is wise to become a people watcher. There is a level of skill involved in this so as not to make it awkward. The idea is not to stare at everyone, but instead to look at and observe those in your environment in a focused and intentional way. When you do this, you will automatically project an aura that you are not an ideal target, which I will discuss later. But more importantly, you will learn to detect important clues and "pre-attack indicators" that could truly be the difference between avoiding a tragedy or being taken completely by surprise. In the next paragraph, I will specifically highlight some of the activities and mannerisms that should raise some suspicion as you observe the people around you. Every one of these is an indicator that I would look for while actively patrolling throughout the years.

First, observe if someone is noticeably looking around. This is something that is often done by an attacker for a few key reasons. Essentially, the attacker may be mentally making a "dry run" at their crime. They may be scanning the area to see how many potential witnesses are around. They may also be looking for ideal approach and escape routes after they finish the attack, or even weapons of opportunity to help carry out the attack. In addition to looking around, I observe if someone is paying an excessive amount of attention to me or anyone else in the area. If there is a good reason for the attention, such as that person is making a lot of noise or acting in a weird manner, this does not apply. But, if there is no reasonable explanation for someone to be focused on a person, this is a possible concern. Finally, look for clothing abnormalities or frequent clothing adjustments. For example, if it is a balmy eighty degrees, someone wearing a jacket or other heavy clothing warrants some level of suspicion. There may be a reasonable explanation, or they may be concealing a weapon. Furthermore, frequent physical adjustments to clothing, particularly near the waistband area, is a common indicator of someone concealing a weapon. There are many other mannerisms, behaviors, or physical acts that can be considered pre-attack indicators: stretching, glancing at a target, verbal threats, clenched fists, and threatening postures to name a few. You will no doubt discover additional indicators as you begin to make this a practice. But on a final but critical note: NONE of these individual indicators alone are enough to warrant action. They are merely indicators that should pique your curiosity and attention to be ready for the potential of an attack. The more indicators you have, the more elevated your level of preparation should be.

As I have already shared, a concept I consistently re-iterate with students is to resist the urge to rationalize away their hunches. Once again, trust your instincts. I am not sure I can adequately describe how important this simple concept is to your safety. When you get the feeling that something, or someone, or some situation is not right, listen to that feeling. I believe it is your subconscious mind observing some of the previously mentioned indicators and letting you know that it is observing danger. It is up to your conscious mind to listen to it.

This concept resonates extremely well with my students. I cannot recount how many times students have relayed stories about situations in which they ignored multiple pre-attack indicators. Through the years I have shared some of these stories with other students and even described some of them in my last book. It is something that can happen to anyone of us no matter how "tactical" we think we are. Just being aware that we as humans are constantly fighting the urge to "normalize" everything we see is a step in the right direction. It is okay to be suspicious! Recognizing this is without question one of the key components to your safety.

Next, I want to address two concepts that will automatically make you less likely to be a target. First, is intentional eye contact. I know there are differences of opinion on the value of eye contact but in my experience, I firmly believe that eye contact sends an unmistakable signal that you are not an easy target. Furthermore, it means you are less likely to be taken by surprise. I teach all of my students the value of eye contact. The second concept is in all environments, try to gravitate toward the position of advantage. What I mean is when you position yourself in a room, at a restaurant, at a movie theater, or wherever else you may be, try to position yourself so that you have multiple escape routes, a field of view that allows you to see people approaching you, and a difficult position for people to approach you from behind. Good eye contact, plus a position of advantage is an outstanding way to avoid an attack altogether, but in a worst-case scenario, be as prepared as possible if one does occur.

Up to this point, I have discussed a myriad of ways to increase your awareness level and how to watch for a potential attacker. Now I want to piece it all together with one final tip in this arena. Reverse roles. Ask yourself if you were the attacker, how easy of a target would you be? This can be uncomfortable for people, but what better way to prepare yourself for defense than by putting yourself in the place of someone who would want to harm you? What could you learn by doing this? Really attempt to view your actions, body language, and practices from the opposite perspective. When you do, I guarantee that you will develop an awareness level that is above and beyond that of the average person.

A chapter about mindset, awareness, and developing the mental edge would not be complete without addressing mental health. I am in no way a mental health professional and will not claim to understand all aspects of this issue. However, in a twenty-year career in law enforcement, I have seen first how incredibly important mental health is to personal defense. More police officers succumb to suicide each year than are killed in the line of duty. Right now I know more is being done now than at any other time in history to address what many are referring to as a "mental health crisis" in first responder fields.

In the past, there was a negative stigma attached to suicide and mental health in general. In my experience incredible advances are being made in this area, and this perception is changing. There is still a lot of work to be done. But for anyone reading this it is critical to remember that you matter, people need you, and there is help available to get you to a state of positive and thriving mental health.

Finally, I would like to share with you an experience that helped me put mindset and attitude into perspective. The lesson learned that day not only stayed with me, but I have applied it to numerous areas of life. One particular day I sent a message to one of my mentors, explaining that I was really experiencing quite a bit of bad luck. Within minutes, he called me and told me a story, which I later learned was known as the parable of the Taoist Farmer. If you have not heard this story it goes as follows:

There once was a farmer whose only horse broke out of his corral and ran off. All of the farmer's neighbors heard what happened and expressed their sympathy to him for having such bad luck. The farmer replied to their concern by saying, "Bad luck, good luck, maybe, who knows?"

A few days later, the farmer's horse returned. But when the horse returned, it was companied by an entire herd of wild horses. The farmer and his son corralled the horses, and once again all of the farmer's neighbors came to see him. This time, they expressed their amazement at how lucky the farmer was. The farmer replied to their comments by saying, "Bad luck, good luck, maybe, who knows?"

While riding one of the wild horses, the farmer's son fell off and broke his leg. Yet again, the farmer's neighbors heard what happened and expressed their sympathy to him for having such bad luck. The farmer replied to their concern by saying, "Bad luck, good luck, maybe, who knows?"

The next day, a war broke out between a rival village and all able-bodied young men were recruited to fight. The farmer's son, unable to fight because of the broken leg, was spared from going to war.

The lesson I learned from the story was that although we cannot control everything that happens around us, our perspective is imperative in terms of how we view the events in our lives. The truth is so many times when we think something is terrible, it turns out to be a "blessing in disguise." I am so happy to not only have this perspective but to have mentors willing to share important lessons with me when I need them.

In this chapter, we talked about a self-defense mindset in a variety of aspects. But we only scratched the surface in terms of how important your mind is to your personal defense. This was designed to be a foundation to build from, but I encourage to constantly find ways to develop a mental edge in your personal protection strategies. This first part of this chapter was not meant to scare or discourage you, but rather encourage to develop or continue to emphasize a self-defense mindset. Tactical breathing and striving to be present in the moment are key. The middle of the chapter was designed to help you enhance your tools of observation and make yourself an undesirable target of the attack. Finally, the end of the chapter was structured in a way to share with you how pivotal perspective and attitude is in terms of self-defense and all of life in general. As I said in the beginning of the chapter, your mind is your single greatest survival tool.

At the end of each chapter of this book, I will attach a "Most Important Concepts" section. Not only to reinforce the most essential principles discussed but also so you can use it as a convenient reference to come back to strengthen and remind you of the key points on your path of personal defense mastery.

Chapter 1 Most Important Concepts

- ➤ Use slow, controlled, deep breathing to manage stress and the challenges you face
- ➤ Strive to be more present in the moment
- ➤ Mentally rehearse positive outcomes in a variety of scenarios
- ➤ Critically review what you do and continuously strive to improve
- ➤ Keep training exciting, different, and enjoyable
- ➤ You are your primary competition
- ➤ Awareness of both your environment and the people in it is critical for self-defense
- ➤ Learn to trust your instincts
- ➤ View yourself and your actions from the perspective of an attacker

> Your mental health is critical for personal defense

Perspective is everything, remember the parable of the Taoist Farmer

Chapter 2 - Defensive Driving

A tree never hits an automobile except in self-defense. ~American Proverb

For almost everyone reading this book right now, statistically speaking, the most dangerous thing you have done today or even this week, is either driven or been a passenger in a motor vehicle. Until technology has progressed to the point that modes of transportation are operated by something other than humans, this will likely be the case. Nearly every adult has known someone, or have themselves been profoundly affected by the death of someone they care about by way of a vehicle accident. Yet, at the time of this writing, how many drivers on the road are distracted by any number of things to include cell phones, mechanisms within the vehicle, or even the lunch they are eating? Virtually every one of us agrees that driving is a potentially dangerous endeavor, yet so many of us are not as focused and mentally present during the operation of our vehicles as we know we should be. Because of this, I knew it was essential to include this chapter in a book dedicated to personal safety.

If you drive down any interstate, freeway, highway, city street, or gravel road for any reasonable length of time, you will inevitably see wooden crosses off the shoulders and embankments. These crosses serve as memorials for the family and friends who have lost their loved ones in vehicle tragedies on our public roads. To paint an even more somber picture, for every intersection and side street that has a wooden cross, there are likely ten more that have been the locations of deadly accidents that are not marked. Only the immediate family and friends of the deceased, as well as the police and fire personnel that responded to the scene, have any memory of the tragedy that occurred in those places.

In twenty years of law enforcement experience, several of those years on patrol as a deputy and sergeant, as well as a few years on the Accident Investigation Unit, I have seen the immediate aftermath of vehicle fatalities on more occasions than most people would imagine. Multiple vehicle deaths, pedestrians hit by vehicles, vehicles against trees, houses, and trains or even cars fully immersed in bodies of water. As I am certain that you would expect, although each of these scenes is horrible on their own accord, the absolute worst of these involved children.

The good news is I am not going to describe or recall my experiences with those deadly scenes in this chapter. Instead, I am going to detail the most important skills, tips, and tactics I have learned about safe driving over the years as a patrol deputy, patrol sergeant, lieutenant, accident investigator, and emergency and defensive driving instructor for my agency.

Over the last several years in my courses, whether it is a firearms course or an empty hand self-defense course, I often bring up the importance of safe vehicle operation. The statement I make usually goes something like this: "I think it is great that you are here learning to defend yourself against a mugger, active shooter, etc. but did you know that if you were to be killed in the next two weeks, it is exponentially more likely that it will happen in your car?" Then I look around the room at my students as most of them nod their heads in recognition of the fact that being killed in an automobile is all too common of an experience in our culture.

But here is the most frustrating, mind-boggling, and at the same time amazing thing of all: It does not have to be that way! Vehicle "accidents" are overwhelmingly avoidable. Overwhelmingly. In my experience in responding to hundreds of vehicle collisions, I have never responded to one that was truly a mechanical

43

failure that was completely unforeseeable and unpreventable. I will concede that these types of incidents do occur, but they are exceptionally rare. Armed with that knowledge alone, we have the responsibility to do everything possible to become the safest drivers we can be. If we do this, not only will we substantially decrease the likelihood that we will be in an accident, we will also play a role in making everyone else on the road a little safer as well.

The concepts, skills, and ideas I will layout in this chapter are the culmination of multiple driving instructor schools as well as lessons learned through collision investigation and response. As with virtually everything in the personal defense realm, unique incidents and situations are fluid and there are exceptions to even the strictest rules. But I guarantee the following concepts have been proven to be instrumental in avoiding not only fatality accidents but non-injury accidents as well. Anyone who has ever been involved in any type of accident will tell you, if it can be avoided, then do it at all costs!

Before getting into the more advanced concepts, I want to start things off simple. Safety equipment and maintenance checks are essential and there is no room for negotiation. As I have stated, the vast majority of vehicular deaths are avoidable, and the first and most significant step you can take is to make sure to routinely completing the following: check the air in your tires, make sure you have a functional spare tire, know how to place the spare tire on your vehicle if the need were to arise, wear your seatbelt, adjust your mirrors, and check the functionality of your lights and signals. These basic safety and equipment checks lay a solid foundation for safe driving. Make them habitual for you.

Once you know and understand the basics, it is important to recognize the most common contributing factors to accidents. They are the following: speed, distraction, and fatigue. I would challenge you to look at collision reports anywhere in the world, and I would safely bet that one or more of those three things were listed as contributing factors. The critical thing to take away is that each of these things can be controlled by the driver. The speed of the vehicle is completely determined by the driver. The amount of focus on the task at hand is also determined by the driver. Finally, while sometimes more difficult to manage, the level of fatigue experienced by the driver is not completely out of control. Although this seems simple and appears to be common sense, these factors cause multiple accidents, including deadly ones, every single day. Armed with this knowledge, you can consciously focus on controlling these factors every time you drive, rather than be controlled by them. Again, if this sounds easy that is because it is. But a word of caution, it is easy to disregard these three controllable factors as well.

Speaking of controllable factors, two additional things that cause deadly accidents at an alarming rate. Virtually everyone knows it, yet they still happen every day and night on our roadways. I am talking about drinking alcohol or using drugs and driving, and texting and driving. Again, it is simple and common sense, but these two violations kill people every day. To be a safe driver, it is imperative that you not only avoid these activities at all costs but also insist that others avoid them as well. It is a cause worth advocating for.

Now that we have talked about the contributing factors to accidents that you must avoid, it is time to discuss the positive driving habits you should develop. First, and arguably foremost, is visual recognition. Defensive driving is based upon seeing what you should be seeing, in the way you should be seeing it. I literally cannot count how many times I have heard a driver involved in an accident say, "I did not see them coming" or "That car just came out of nowhere." Obviously, the car did not just materialize magically out of nowhere, rather the driver did not see the other vehicle in time. This is such an important concept to understand in terms of safe driving.

In various driving instructor courses, I have heard theories of why people see the way they do when they drive, as well as how they should be applying their vision to driving. Some suggest that because the natural mode of transportation for human beings is walking, we tend to look only a few feet in front of us, rather than several hundred feet in the distance. Others suggest that we should not glance far into the distance because this could lead to "highway hypnosis" due to the monotonous highway lines. What I have found to be most effective in safe driving is a combination of viewing much farther into the distance than you might think, coupled with changing what you are looking at consistently. I think there is tremendous value in viewing into the distance in terms of being able to detect possible upcoming hazards in the quickest amount of time possible. Furthermore, consistently changing your focus and field of view will not only help you perceive the environment around you but will help combat the aforementioned "highway hypnosis." In terms of safe driving, focusing on seeing the world around you in a larger, more deliberate way, is quite possibly the most important thing you can do.

In addition to seeing what you need to see, creating a cushion of space in every direction around your vehicle is vitally important. This will aid you in seeing and scanning the road around you, but more importantly, it will create reaction time to unforeseen events, as well as create opportunities for "escape routes" to help you avoid collisions with other vehicles. In addition, this will limit vehicles being in the "blind spots" of your car. Seeing a large field of view coupled with constantly creating space around your vehicle will decrease your likelihood of getting into an accident exponentially. One of my driving instructors said to me, "It is best to be an anti-social driver." What he meant by that was that drivers have a tendency to travel in clusters with other cars. Furthermore, our traffic signals tend to group cars into clusters as part of the natural flow of movement. But the safe, intelligent, and properly positioned driver does not travel within these clusters, but rather within the space created between the clusters of cars. The genius thing about this mindset is not only does this result in the driver being less likely to be in a collision with another vehicle, the driver also tends to get stuck at red lights at a substantially lower rate. I encourage you to test this out for yourself. I think you will be amazed when you discover your overall driving experience will not only be safer, but less stressful as well.

Before getting into the essentials of skilled driving, I want to address certain special circumstances when it comes to driving. First, the risk posed by inclement weather. It is astounding the number of vehicle collisions of all types that occur in the snow, rain, high winds or any other weather event. Almost without exception, these collisions could be completely avoided by reducing speed. There is no secret whatsoever to the primary way to avoid accidents in adverse conditions. Reducing speed is the definitive answer. There is something to be said about knowing the differences in maneuvering a vehicle in wet or icy conditions, as well as understanding the braking system on the vehicle to avoid locking up the brakes or skidding and sliding. I will get into the essentials of vehicle maneuvering later in the chapter, but again all of this is secondary to the reduction of speed in inclement weather.

The second special circumstance that is worthy of discussion is collisions with animals. As a deputy sheriff in the state of Kansas, responding to vehicles colliding with deer is an extremely common occurrence. But deer are not the only animals that pose a problem on roadways. Cows, horses, even dogs have been involved with everything from minor accidents to fatality accidents. In my experience with literally hundreds of accidents involving cars and animals, the most common reason the accident becomes more serious is that the driver attempted to evade the animal. This often results in an even worse collision when the driver completely loses control and strikes another vehicle or object. To be clear, if there is a clear escape route to avoid the collision altogether, that is the best option. But, oftentimes reducing speed, but remaining in the same lane even it means striking the animal, is the safest option. Every situation is different and fluid, but this is certainly something to keep in mind.

The next special circumstance worth addressing is incidents that occur on the side of the roadway. Police officers, tow truck drivers, and stranded motorists are killed every year in a multitude of accidents that occur on the shoulders of the roadways. Distraction and overall inattention are the primary causes of this type of collision. However, impaired drivers are also a common culprit. Two of my scariest moments as a patrol deputy were on the shoulders of a 70 MPH speed limit state highway. The first was a drunk driver who came within inches of hitting me during a traffic stop, and the second was a distracted driver who slammed on her brakes and lost control into a full three hundred and sixty-degree circle around my patrol car when she realized how close she was to the car in front of her.

Fortunately, I am alive to write about these incidents and share the stories in the hope that one of my readers or students will take the lessons learned and be part of the solution to help avoid future events like this. Unfortunately, a deputy that I worked with for many years was killed while sitting in his patrol car during a traffic stop. The driver was intoxicated, and everything about the senseless loss of the life of that extremely well-liked deputy was avoidable. Master Deputy Brandon Collins was a knowledgeable officer who was genuinely loved and admired by not only those within my agency but officers and agents from several other law enforcement organizations. The impact of his line of duty death has been felt by his family, friends, and the community. Every year, along with friends of Brandon and knowledgeable firearms enthusiasts, I serve as the match director for the Brandon Collins Memorial Shootout. This is an all skill level event, the proceeds for which are given directly to a first responder family in need. As of this writing, the 2019 match proceeds went to the families of two deputies who were murdered in the line of duty. Please follow and support this incredible event on the various social media pages under Brandon Collins Memorial Shootout.

The last special circumstance I want to discuss regarding driving is road rage. Multiple studies have been done on this phenomenon and if you watch the local news for no more than just a few weeks there is an extremely high likelihood that you will see one or more incidents involving road rage. Many times, the outcome of the event is tragic. I often include in my classes a news article I discovered in which two drivers were involved in a road rage situation that escalated into one of the drivers shooting into the vehicle of the other driver while at a stoplight. Neither of the drivers was physically injured; however, the three-year-old daughter of one of the drivers was killed while in the back seat.

There are no winners in road rage situations, and there are no positive outcomes. Countless lives have been forever changed in horrific ways because of a conflict on the road with someone they had never previously met in their entire lives. The bottom line is this: Avoid being a part of road rage incidents at all costs. It is the safest and most intelligent thing you can do. If you see an incident start to materialize, slow down, back off, change routes, and do not take part in it. That is the correct decision and it is worth it. The next time you sense any type of aggressive driving on the roadway and you feel like it is affecting you, create distance, use the controlled, deep breathing discussed in the previous chapter, and avoid this type of confrontation.

Now that we have discussed the importance of safe driving, the essential tips in terms of equipment checks, vision, and space between vehicles, and some special circumstances on the roadway, I would like to discuss some of the actual driving skills that all good drivers should become proficient at. These include understanding "blind spots" to your position, handling the "right of way" appropriately, safely driving at night, maneuvering through curves and turns, and understanding the transfer of weight of a vehicle in motion.

Many collisions are the result of one driver not seeing another vehicle due to it being in the "blind spot." More and more vehicle mirrors and cameras are decreasing these blind spots but it is incumbent upon the driver to know where these blind spots exist and actively adjust their speed and position to minimize them. As I mentioned earlier, consciously striving to create a cushion of space among other vehicles will help with this as well.

Another common cause of collisions is one driver failing to yield the right of way to another vehicle. While this is extremely common, even if the collision is not your fault legally, it is still worth avoiding. Because of this, I teach my students to always confirm the right of way is being given to them as opposed to assuming it is.

By doing this, they are much less likely to be involved in this type of collision.

Nighttime driving creates the added challenge of reducing the vision of the driver. We already discussed the importance of vision, so it is important to address the reduced vision with functioning lights and a general reduction in speed. Complicating matters are the other drivers who forget to dim their lights when approaching, obstructing your vision even more! The bottom line with night driving is to reduce your speed and focus on utilizing lights to increase your visibility as much as possible.

When entering a curve, roundabout, or other similar turns, it is important to understand the optimal positioning of your vehicle. Generally speaking, you should enter curves on the outside portion of the lane. As you progress toward the center or apex of the curve you should begin positioning your vehicle toward the inside of the lane. Once past the apex, you should begin positioning back toward the outside of the lane. The natural centrifugal force created during the turning process will assist in this positioning. Furthermore, it is imperative to know the dimensions of your vehicle and work to develop an understanding of visual depth perception and how much clearance you have at various roadway locations.

It is best to make any speed adjustments (braking or accelerating) before entering a curve, as opposed to while you are making the turn. Braking/accelerating and steering through a turn at the same time is not the most efficient way to maneuver a vehicle. Once past the apex of the curve, it is okay to begin to accelerate if there is a need to increase your speed. One final tip on curves and turns in general: The rear wheels track to the inside of the vehicle when turning. Because of this, it is important to understand when making a turn it is essential to leave enough space for both the front and rear wheels to stay in the lane. When you do not do this, the very common "curb check" is usually the result.

The next driving tip involves the general maneuverability of your vehicle. First and foremost, you are a better driver with more control when both hands are on the steering wheel. Next, it is important to know how the weight of a motor vehicle shifts depending upon what the driver is doing. When you accelerate, the weight of the vehicle begins to transfer toward the rear. When you brake or decelerate, the weight of the vehicle transfers to the front. The faster the acceleration and more aggressively the brakes are applied, the more dramatic the transfer of weight becomes. The reason this is nice to know is because whichever end of the vehicle the weight is transferring away from, is the more likely end of the vehicle that begins spinning out of control. When that happens, a skilled driver should adjust their speed to regain control of their vehicle.

I now want to share with you a tip on driving that you can begin using immediately. It is one of the most simple and quite honestly game-changing tactics I have ever used in both everyday travel and criminal patrol. Every time you stop, leave at least one car length between you and the car in front of you. I know this sounds so simple, and maybe even unnecessary, but hear me out. First, doing this creates a potential escape route. This could be for something as innocuous as the car in front of you breaking down, or something even more dangerous such as a potential carjacking. Second, if the car in front of you begins unintentionally backing, this extra space may prevent a collision. Third, if you do happen to be rear-ended by the car behind you, this space may be enough to prevent the chain reaction type of collision in which multiple vehicles are involved. Finally, this space will help to increase your view of the environment around you. There are other advantages for sure, and I can assure you once you make this simple procedure a habit, you will discover many of your own additional benefits.

Finally, a chapter dedicated to safe driving would not be complete without a mention of backing your vehicle up. Many accidents occur during the backing process. Some minor, yet some with devastating consequences especially when a young child is the victim. There are many strategies you can use in addition to mirrors and physically turning to look back. Having a passenger direct you if available and slowly proceeding with caution is an option. Also, using the horn as a warning and the technology of back up cameras. Any options available to your disposal to make backing safer are worth it.

There is a lot more to say about general driving safety, the mechanics of good driving, eliminating distractions, and how important every driver on the road is to improving the safety of our transit system. But I think this chapter covered the most essential details and hopefully re-emphasized how and why safe driving is absolutely part of your overall personal defense. Many people are under the impression they are good drivers simply because they have not caused an accident. But while a good driver may not cause accidents, a great driver is someone who, utilizing the knowledge and skills obtained in this chapter, can avoid accidents that would have been caused by other drivers as well. The world desperately needs more great drivers!

Throughout this book, I plan to share with you many of the articles I have written in the last two years for various publications. Many of these articles were the result of conversations with students and are illustrations of the concepts in which I intend to help you learn, grow, and develop from reading this book. Furthermore, you will see repetitive concepts in my defensive strategies, which is completely by design. I would like to start with an article I wrote that was first released in December of 2019 in PoliceOne Magazine. The primary audience for this article initially was law enforcement, but one of the many things I have discovered through the years is that skills traditionally thought of as meant for police officers only, are also ideal for the safety of everyday citizens. In fact, more citizens should learn the basic safety and awareness principles taught to law enforcement as this would make all of us safer. Some of this article recaps what we have discussed here, but it also connects self-defense with defensive driving which is one of the underlying themes of this book.

The Connection between Defensive Tactics and Defensive Driving

Why Making Connections Matters During Police Training

(Featured in PoliceOne December 4th, 2019)

Today's police officer wears a lot of hats and, as a result, receives training in multiple areas. Because of this, many agencies resort to a "block and silo" approach to training. In other words, a block of training is dedicated to each topic until officers are inundated with information about everything from firearms to de-escalation, first aid to defensive tactics.

The downside to this style of training is that it can be difficult for officers to see how the skills they learn during each training block complement each other. In virtually every call for service, officers need to use multiple skills, so why aren't we training cops that way?

One way to address this police training deficit is to make connections between the various skills we train officers in through studying concepts that overlap those skills. In this article, I would like to connect two high-profile training topics that are paramount to officer and citizen safety: Defensive tactics and defensive driving.

The Reactionary Gap and the Space Cushion

Most agencies train officers to understand the value of maintaining a sufficient reactionary gap when dealing with potentially volatile subjects. Although it's not always feasible, extra caution should be exhibited when someone is within the appropriate reactionary gap (usually closer than six to eight feet).

This same concept is taught in the context of defensive driving, and for many of the same reasons. When driving, leaving a sufficient amount of space between the officer's car and the vehicle in front of them gives them additional time to respond to rapidly evolving situations.

Equipment Checks

Prior to their shift starting, officers are trained to inspect the various defensive tools they have on their duty belt or load-bearing vest. They are also trained to inspect their vehicles to ensure they have the required equipment and are functional. In both cases, these checks could contribute to a successful resolution to a serious situation or help avoid a vehicle accident.

Disengagement Options and Escape Routes

In defensive tactics training, officers are taught to evaluate when to disengage as an option. This could be to deploy a tool or wait for backup officers.

In defensive driving, the driver is taught to locate potential escape routes in the event of an abrupt stop or other hazard they may be confronted with on the roadway.

Either way, these two valuable concepts apply to both topics.

Maintaining Control

In both disciplines, an extremely important concept is the ability of the officer to maintain reasonable control over the situation. This translates into a higher likelihood of a successful resolution.

In defensive tactics, a well-trained officer maintaining control is less likely to use excessive force in a given incident. In defensive driving, maintaining control of the vehicle is essential to avoid collisions.

In both of these cases, it isn't necessarily the "toughest" officer or the officer who can drive the fastest that succeeds, but instead the officer who understands how to maintain control of the situation.

Knowing Laws and Policies

Knowing relevant use-of-force laws, as well as traffic laws, is an absolute must. Furthermore, officers must be extremely familiar with their individual department's policy on these topics. This not only improves their ability to make safe and reasonable decisions, it protects them from liability in these two oftentimes hotly contested subjects.

Recognizing recurring themes in police training is valuable because it helps officers use general concepts from one area of training, and subsequently apply them to other areas they may not be as familiar with. Training becomes more relevant and impactful when an officer realizes they can take the tools and skills they learn in one area and use it in a variety of contexts, which helps maximize training time and improve overall officer efficiency.

Train hard and be safe!

Chapter 2 Most Important Concepts

- Becoming a defensive driver is one of the most important things you can do for the safety of you and your family
- Make it a priority to check the equipment and functionality of your vehicle
- Speed, distractions, and fatigue are controllable factors that are involved in most collisions
- Impaired driving and texting while driving are absolute recipes for disaster
- Inclement weather, collisions with animals, and side of the roadway accidents are special circumstances that should be thought about beforehand in an attempt to avoid
- There are no winners in road rage incidents; avoid them at all costs
- Look both ahead into the distance and scan your peripheral to increase your

vision and field of view when driving

➤ Awareness of both your environment and the people in it is critical for self-defense

➤ Manage blind spots, always confirm the right of way, and reduce speed and utilize lights effectively during night time driving

➤ Understand the maneuverability of your particular vehicle and how the weight transfers and shifts during driving

➤ Leave at least one car length of space between you and the car in front of you when stopped

➤ A good driver does not cause collisions, but a great driver also avoids collisions caused by others

➤ Personal defense arenas are interrelated, as described in the article

Chapter 3 - Empty Hand Self-Defense

Always assume that your opponent is going to be bigger, stronger and faster than you; so that you learn to rely on technique, timing, and leverage rather than brute strength. –Helio Gracie

When I was five years old, my mother introduced me to a movie that unbeknownst to me would turn out to be one of the most significant catalysts in shaping the future of my life. In this movie, a smaller statured Chinese guy used a combination of kicks and punches to defeat all his adversaries. The movie was *Enter the Dragon* and the star was Bruce Lee. When my mom asked if I wanted to learn martial arts, there was no doubt in my mind. So at the age of five, I began my journey into what has become a decades' long study, love, and appreciation for the martial arts.

I lived in Hawaii at the time, and my first style of martial arts was known as *Shito-Ryu,* which is a traditional Japanese style of martial arts that involves powerful kicks, punches, and strikes of various types. Martial arts became a staple of my childhood and I progressed through the ranks and competed in tournaments throughout my childhood years.

My family eventually moved to the Midwest, where I continued to train and began teaching martial arts under my step-father, who was a black belt in *Shito-Ryu.* Instead of competitive team sports, I spent most of my junior high and high school weekends competing in karate tournaments throughout the Midwest.

A childhood of martial arts training is something that I cannot speak highly enough about. There is a reason why so many martial artists encourage others to enroll their children in martial arts to develop character, respect, discipline, confidence, self-defense abilities and more.

If my introduction to martial arts by way of the classic movie *Enter the Dragon* was the most defining moment into my study of martial arts, then the second most significant moment came at the age of sixteen. November 11th, 1993 to be exact. This was the date of the first-ever Ultimate Fighting Championship. My entire martial arts academy gathered together to watch this event live on a big-screen television. The premise of this event was simple; gather together fighters of different styles of martial arts to include Boxing, Tae Kwon Do, Sumo Wrestling, Kenpo, Shootfighting, Gracie Jiu-Jitsu, etc. and have them compete one on one with virtually no rules and see who would emerge victoriously. For years martial arts enthusiasts had speculated which "style" of martial art would fare better in a no-rules fight. But for the first time, an event like that was put together for a worldwide audience. If you have not seen the original UFC, I suggest searching for a copy and viewing it.

What happened that night was one of the most defining events in martial arts history. At twenty-six years old and one hundred and seventy-eight pounds, one of the smallest and most unassuming fighters in the competition defeated his opponents one after another on the same night to become the first UFC Champion. Royce Gracie represented the now famous Gracie Family and their art which was adapted and derived from the traditional Japanese arts of Judo and Jiu-Jitsu. Focused primarily on the ground aspect of fighting, Gracie Jiu-Jitsu uses timing, technique, and leverage to achieve a dominant position and end the encounter by applying a joint lock or stranglehold to the opponent. In contrast, most martial arts rely primarily on speed, strength, and violence of action to accomplish their objective.

This was the beginning of a definitive shift in traditional thinking in terms of what effective hand to hand martial arts were, and how they apply to self-defense. For generations, the population was trained through visual displays of combat sports or other "fights" that the correct way to engage in physical combat was for two people to exchange strikes until one person knocked out their opponent. But when two people are within striking range of each other, even with a significant amount of training, a larger aggressor always has a chance to connect with a devastating strike to a smaller person. By changing the "rules" of what a fight should look like, Gracie Jiu-Jitsu has given a substantial advantage to the smaller and less athletic person. This was and is game-changing.

Fast forward nearly three decades later to the time of this writing, the UFC has become a multi-billion dollar industry that features the most elite fighters in the world. To be successful, every single one of them has to know how to fight on the ground. At the extreme minimum, the fighters in the UFC must have an extremely high level of defense against takedowns and the ability to get back up if taken to the ground.

You have probably heard someone say, "Most fights go to the ground." The reason you have heard this is because it is true. If you analyze most fights, as I have through years of law enforcement and martial arts practice, you will find that most fights do go to the ground. I would also suggest that many that do not, fall into the unique category of the well-timed, well placed, or even flat out lucky, "quick knock out."

Now I know that the majority of people reading this do not have any ambitions of becoming the next UFC Champion, but I wanted to set the framework for training Gracie Jiu-Jitsu, and why it has been my martial art of choice for well over a decade. To be clear, I think there is great value in virtually all martial arts, with the person's goals, personality, and physical characteristics all being significant factors in terms of which one is best for them.

I will highlight the primary reasons that Gracie Jiu-Jitsu as a personal empty hand self-defense art is so effective in the following paragraphs. First, Gracie Jiu-Jitsu works. Even prior to the UFC, the Gracie Family gained a large following and notoriety through what was referred to as the "Gracie Challenge." They issued a running challenge to other martial artists to do something that not many others were actually willing to do. They put their money where their mouths were. Time and after time, the Gracie family members or their representatives emerged victorious when challenged.

Next, as I stated earlier, Gracie Jiu-Jitsu relies on technique, timing, and leverage as the keys to victory, rather than speed, size, and strength. This is of critical importance because, in a self-defense encounter, there are no weight classes. One of the basic tenets of traditional self-defense Gracie Jiu-Jitsu is to always assume that your opponent is going to be bigger, stronger, and faster than you are. I often joke with my students in class that if dispatch sends me to a disturbance, it would be great if I could ask what size the suspect was, and only go if he or she was in my weight class. The class usually follows with laughter and concedes the point that relying on size and strength has quite a few limitations.

Gracie Jiu-Jitsu relies primarily on natural body movements and energy efficiency. This is also important because any martial art that requires extreme flexibility or athleticism is not going to be useful for everyone, and over time will be less useful for even the best practitioners. Furthermore, because becoming skilled at Gracie Jiu-Jitsu requires the practitioner to learn to be efficient with their energy and movements, it is something that can be trained well into "old age."

Finally, a unique aspect of Gracie Jiu-Jitsu is that you can control a much bigger and stronger opponent with substantially less force than nearly every other martial art. The benefit of this is tremendous. Not only can you defend yourself, but in essence, you can do it in a way that causes less injury to the person you are defending yourself from. While this may not seem like a big deal, in a highly litigious society where you can never really be sure what a jury might decide, having the ability to end a physical confrontation with minimal injury to your opponent is a huge deal. Both the adaptability and scalability of Gracie Jiu-Jitsu are two of its greatest strengths.

Throughout the years I have taught Gracie Jiu-Jitsu to police officers, children, women, and just about every demographic you can think of at several martial arts academies. I cannot speak highly enough about its value in terms of improving your ability to defend yourself. I encourage you to find a place to train, and if possible, make it a regular part of your training. Not only is it a fantastic system of self-defense, but also outstanding physical exercise.

One caution that is an important consideration is this: Gracie Jiu-Jitsu, sometimes referred to as Brazilian Jiu-Jitsu, is also rapidly becoming a highly competitive sport. While this is a good thing, it is nice to know if a particular Jiu-Jitsu academy is sport-focused or self-defense focused, or in a few cases both. If you are training for self-defense as your primary motivation, then a school that emphasizes the sportive and competitive aspect of Jiu-Jitsu may not be the best fit. Schools like this tend to focus on the point scoring system and rules of competitive Jiu-Jitsu as opposed to the techniques designed to defeat common threats from an attack in a self-defense scenario. Do not get it twisted, competitive Jiu-Jitsu schools are outstanding and usually comprised of skilled, dedicated athletes. It just may not meet the goals of a self-defense driven student. Conversely, if you wish to explore the sportive aspects of Jiu-Jitsu, then a school focused on self-defense may not be a good fit either.

Before moving on, I want to give credit to the members of the Gracie Family that I have had the honor and privilege of training directly under for years. Not only have they been incredible martial artists, but also mentors and teachers who genuinely care about their students. A large majority of the teaching methodologies and philosophies I use can be attributed directly to what I have learned from the Gracie Family.

Now that I have explained why Gracie Jiu-Jitsu is my martial art of choice, I want to discuss a few of the common myths about self-defense and martial arts in general. So in the following paragraphs, I will discuss these most common self-defense misconceptions that are widely regarded as true.

The first and most common misconception of all time is probably, "I'll just strike the attacker in the groin." The first problem with this is that a well-placed kick or other strike to the groin is much more of a challenge than most people realize, especially under the surprise and duress of a typical fight. Second, although a hit to the groin can be extremely painful, it may not completely end the fight. It may anger the attacker even more and cause a rush of adrenaline adding more conviction and ferocity to the attack. Third, it is an expected attack that opponents tend to be cognizant of. To be clear, groin shots are legitimate attacks that *can* work, and certainly have a place in your overall self-defense strategy. They just are not the fabled "golden bullet" that many people make them out to be.

The next topic I want to address is not so much a misconception, but just a general word of caution. There are a lot of horrible "instructors" and claims about what works in self-defense out there. There just is not a nice way to explain this reality. The internet is filled with self-defense videos of techniques that simply will not work in actual situations. The problem is that it can be difficult for an uninformed person to tell the difference between legitimate techniques and ones that are complete fiction. Couple that with the fact that many of these "instructors" have dynamic personalities and present themselves in a way that makes their students believe what they are teaching is real. This has been one of the long-standing problems with martial arts in general.

A couple of key observations can help you identify if an "instructor" is not legitimate. First, if their approach sounds like a "my way or no way" approach, that should raise suspicion. Martial arts are not a one size fits all proposition, and we all have our preferences and approaches that can accomplish the objective of keeping us safe. Second, if an instructor is not forthcoming about their background in martial arts or does not produce anything verifiable in terms of their rank and training, they are very likely being deceptive. Also, if their martial arts school has any general feeling of being more focused on long term contracts or expensive belt promotions, it is probably not a good place to train. In the martial arts world, we refer to these as "McDojos." In general, if anything at all does not seem right about an instructor or school in terms of legitimacy, costs, or instructor qualifications, then it probably is not. As I discussed in Chapter 1, trust your instincts!

Finally, I want to discuss the practicality of learning self-defense from a seminar. The reality is it is virtually impossible to develop the skill required to defend yourself after attending one seminar. This is not to say that self-defense seminars have no value because they do. However, seminars should only be part of an overall plan to consistently develop your empty hand self-defense skills.

74

I hope that I have encouraged you to embark on the rewarding journey of learning a martial art. I know that joining a martial arts academy can be intimidating, but I guarantee you in most cases the reward outweighs the risk. For every excuse you can think of not to try it, I bet there are better reasons to go for it. While for me Gracie Jiu-Jitsu is the martial art of choice, many other styles might be a better fit for you. But I cannot emphasize enough the value it will bring to your overall self-defense as well as physical and mental health.

If joining a martial arts academy is simply not in the cards for you at this time, then do not worry. Perhaps in the future, it will be. Until then, I think it would be important to at minimum add some flexibility exercises and striking movements to your workouts or at random times throughout the week. This does not have to be time-consuming, with even only a few minutes a few times a week having the potential of being extremely beneficial. You will not always have a gun or other defensive tool immediately available at every moment of the day. But one thing that will always be present if you are physically attacked is you. Having some physical defensive strategies is imperative.

For those of you who want to know the basics of empty-hand self-defense but cannot train

75

martial arts regularly, here are the essentials. First, learn the various distances in a physical fight. It is important to know if you are within kicking distance, punching distance, elbow and knee strike distance, and finally grappling distance. Your defenses change considerably based on distance. Next, develop a good fighting stance. The elements of a good fighting stance are both knees bent, hands up, your stronger side slightly toward the back, and your weight shifted slightly more toward the front. In terms of striking, it is important to recognize that striking with a closed fist, particularly without extensive training, has certain limitations. The damage done to your knuckles can be painful. Instead, with limited training, I usually suggest strikes with an open palm.

Finally, I want to leave you with two tips you can begin using right now to enhance your ability to defend yourself from a physical attack. First, when communicating with someone who you have determined to be a potential threat, begin to work on your position immediately. What you are attempting to gain is an angle off to the side (straight forward attacks are easiest for an aggressor) as well as at least a few feet of distance (this is to increase visibility and reaction time to a threat). Lastly, begin learning to speak with your hands up and in front of you. This will give you a definitive edge in reaction time to defending yourself against a sudden attack. With practice, speaking with your hands up in tense situations will look natural and not aggressive. This skill is something that is routinely taught to police officers around the world.

I would like to end this chapter by sharing with you an article that I wrote for Brazilian Jiu-Jitsu Eastern Europe appearing in April of 2019 that explains how Jiu-Jitsu not only helped me with self-defense but how the concepts I have learned from it have also applied to life.

Five Things You Learn on the Mat that Apply to Life

(Featured in Brazilian Jiu-Jitsu Eastern Europe August 22nd, 2019)

So many of us love Jiu-Jitsu because of the benefits we derive from being on the mat. From the camaraderie to the health benefits, to the competition aspects and more. But one of the most amazing things I have discovered in the last ten years of the training is that the lessons learned on the mat carry over to life in several meaningful ways. Here are five examples of things you learn on the mat that directly correspond to lessons in life.

One-The more time you spend dealing with uncomfortable positions, the more comfortable you become dealing with adversity. Everyone who trains Jiu-Jitsu for any amount of time knows that when you first begin rolling with your partners, you spend a lot of time in inferior or uncomfortable positions. As you continue to train and gain experience, you gradually become more confident that you will be able to persevere through these positions. Once you realize the power of this principle, everyday problems in life become more manageable.

Two-Timing and leverage are the keys to coming out ahead in situations. On the mat, you quickly learn that while you may be correctly performing the mechanics of a move, it still might not work for you. It is then that you realize that sometimes it is not the move itself that is incorrect, but rather the time or angle at which you are applying is wrong.

Three-Being flexible and adaptable are more important than being rigid and stubborn. While there is something to be said for being persistent, it is a whole different thing entirely being stubborn and unwilling to adapt on the mat. How many times have you seen a beginner try unsuccessfully to finish a submission that is simply not working only to miss out on an opening for another one? Yet again, this is a principle that when applied to life outside of the mat can open many doors and opportunities.

Four-Time and dedication pay off. One thing that many black belts consistently say is that the secret to Jiu-Jitsu is to just keep showing up. I think this is a testament to dedication. There are many ups and downs in Jiu-Jitsu. There are great training days and there are bad ones. But by continuing to be out there day after day and persevering through the many challenges you will face, eventually, positive results will come.

Five-Being humble and respectful to others is the key to meaningful relationships. One of the incredible things about Jiu-Jitsu is that some of the most skilled and dangerous people on the planet are also the most humble and unassuming. Because of this, many people are drawn to them and amazed by their calm and friendly demeanors. This is just one of many reasons why members of the Jiu-Jitsu family can travel around the world and instantly connect with one another.

Jiu-Jitsu provides so many of us an unparalleled joy on the mat. It continues to grow and is rapidly becoming one of the most popular martial arts around. But what is even more amazing than the benefits we get on the mat, is all of the benefits Jiu-Jitsu provides to our everyday lives!

Chapter 3 Most Important Concepts

- ➢ There is tremendous benefit in adding hand to hand self-defense into your personal defense strategy
- ➢ Gracie Jiu-Jitsu is a martial art that relies on technique, timing, and leverage as opposed to strength and athleticism
- ➢ There are many valuable and effective martial arts styles and schools available
- ➢ Not all self-defense instructors teach effective techniques, even though they may have dynamic personalities
- ➢ There is a lot of misinformation about effective self-defense techniques
- ➢ Trust your instincts

- ➤ Martial arts can be valuable for both physical and mental health
- ➤ If martial arts is not possible now, basic stretches and movements to increase your preparation can be beneficial
- ➤ Learn to increase the distance and create angles from potential threats
- ➤ Learn to communicate with your hands up and ready to react

Chapter 4 - Defensive Tools

You must be shapeless, formless, like water. When you pour water in a cup, it becomes the cup. When you pour water in a bottle, it becomes the bottle. When you pour water in a teapot, it becomes the teapot. Water can drip and it can crash. Become like water my friend. - Bruce Lee

Over the years, one common theme that comes up in topics of discussion in both firearms and empty-hand self-defense courses is the use of self-defense tools and how they apply to overall self-defense. Students frequently inquire about tools such as pepper spray, knives, improvised weapons, canes, TASER/stun guns, batons, kubatons, and more. Many have explained that they either cannot or are unwilling to carry a handgun, but would be willing to carry one of these less-lethal tools for self-defense purposes. Others have explained they would like to carry one of these tools in addition to their handgun as another defensive option. But the most common question I get is, "Which one is best and which one should I carry?"

The funny thing about that question is I could answer one way, and another use of force instructor could answer a different way and we could both be right, or wrong. The best tool to carry is the one that will effectively serve its purpose in a given situation. I realize that is not the answer people want to hear; however, I usually continue that discussion with more information so that my students can have a starting point to do their own research.

In this chapter, I will discuss the most common tools available for self-defense and list out some pros and cons of these particular tools. A twenty-year career in law enforcement has given me a unique opportunity to be a part of situations or analyze videos of many of these tools in actual scenarios. Furthermore, as a law enforcement use of force instructor I could study many of the widely recognized strengths and weaknesses associated with them. My lists are neither exhaustive or without exception, as a lot of it is contingent on the specific self-defense situation.

One of the most commonly used defensive tools is pepper spray. Designed to cause a burning session to the assailant's eyes and a substantial amount of pain, it can be used to temporarily hinder vision while simultaneously making it difficult for the attacker to breathe. There is a varying level of effectiveness with this tool, although I have seen it effectively used multiple times. The following are some of the pros to this tool; it is effective in causing pain to the attacker's eyes, it is fairly simple to use, most models have an effective range of about three to fifteen (various models differ in delivery i.e. foam spray, mist), and it is an inexpensive tool that is usually good for several years. The cons of this tools are that a motivated attacker can fight through the pain (especially if it misses the eyes when deployed), there is a chance of a secondary or inadvertent effect on the "good guy" depending on environment and wind conditions, and dependent upon on where it is carried, it make take several seconds to deploy.

The next defensive tool I would like to discuss is any type of knife. A knife is an interesting tool because not only do they have self-defense applications (in very serious situations where personal safety is in jeopardy), but knives also have many other uses. There are an enormous variety of knives so the following list of pros and cons are something I would apply on a general basis to most knives; knives can be highly effective, knives do not really "malfunction" like other tools might, knives can be easy to store and carry in a variety of locations, and although training with a knife makes sense if you are going to carry it in a self-defense capacity, they are fairly easy to use with minimal training, and as I mentioned earlier knives are a multi-use tool that can be valuable in many ways. Some cons to a knife are that you must be in close proximity to the attacker to use it, the use of a knife is a serious situation so you must be extremely aware of the law governing self-defense to ensure that its use is justifiable, and finally, the potential always exists that you could get cut by accident or have the knife used against you.

TASERS or any type of stun gun or electrical weapon have been throughout the last two decades a fairly popular choice for self-defense. There are quite a few reasons why, here are a few of the pros; they are effective on most people, the mere "arcing" of an electrical device is enough to make most people think twice about proceeding with an attack, and they are fairly simple to use. Some of the cons of electrical weapons are these; they may not be as effective if a subject is wearing heavy clothing, quality models of these tools can sometimes be rather expensive, and anytime water is involved there is a concern when using electrical weapons due to the known conductivity of water.

The next tool I will discuss is a general grouping of any batons, kubatons, sticks, bats, canes, nunchaku or any other similar striking instrument that would fit into this category. While this is a broad range, the pros and cons are fairly self-explanatory. First, they can be used to generate a massive amount of energy to create powerful strikes. Second, they can be used to keep an attacker at bay and not want to get too close to you. Finally, many of these weapons can be improvised from household items such as mops and brooms, or already available such as canes. The cons to this type of weapon are if the attacker sneaks up on you and closes the distance before you realize it, the tactical advantage may be lost. Furthermore, consistent training in the various martial arts that specialize in stick fighting is required to truly be confident in these objects as reliable self-defense tools.

Finally, I would like to discuss improvised weapons or weapons of opportunity. This would include virtually anything accessible to you in your immediate environment that could be used at a moment's notice to your advantage if you were attacked. Examples include chairs, otherwise innocuous office objects such as tape dispensers, pens, books, staplers, etc., environmental objects such as rocks and braches, or even a hot cup of coffee or bottle of water. The truth is to create the survival mindset in an attack situation, you have to be willing to do what it takes to stop the threat. When you are caught by surprise, sometimes finding a weapon of opportunity is exactly what it takes to give you that edge. Although some people have a difficult time viewing common items as potential weapons, this practice may be the difference-maker in emerging victorious against an unprovoked attack against you or your family.

I would like to share with you now a product review I wrote for a use of force tool known as the GLOVE that appeared in PoliceOne in December of 2019. While the GLOVE is not available for the civilian market, the following article illustrates some of the principles I have discussed so far in this chapter and describes the process in which I go about analyzing self-defense tools:

First look: The GLOVE use of force tool from Compliant Technologies

(Featured in PoliceOne December 30th, 2019)

When the pads of the GLOVE come into direct contact with human skin, it generates pain compliance.

Over the past few months, I have had the opportunity to test and evaluate a new use of force tool released in May 2019.

The GLOVE, which stands for Generated Low Output Voltage Emitter, is a conducted electrical weapon (CEW) from Compliant Technologies. It is designed to be used in conjunction with an officer's defensive tactics training and other use of force tools to more effectively de-escalate use of force incidents and bring non-compliant subjects under control in a safe and timely manner.

How the GLOVE works

The GLOVE can be worn both before and during a law enforcement contact in correctional and field settings. When needed, the GLOVE is turned on by depressing the on/off button located on the upper surface of the GLOVE. When the tool is turned on, the on button illuminates in a manner that is highly visible to the officer.

There are conductive electrode pads on the palm side of the GLOVE. When two of these pads come into direct contact with human skin, it generates pain compliance and achieves neural peripheral interference. The desired result of the GLOVE is to cause a distraction to the peripheral nervous system, making it more difficult for the subject to perform coordinated muscle movement. This distraction then allows the officer to place the subject under control.

The primary target areas of the GLOVE are the extremities and joints. Unless it is an escalated situation to defend someone from serious bodily harm, applying the GLOVE to a subject's head, face, throat, or groin area is not recommended.

Testing of the GLOVE

After completing a one-day master instructor course, I began conducting tests of the GLOVE with other law enforcement instructors.

The testing included multiple trips to the firing range to determine if the GLOVE can be worn in the on or off position when transitioning and using other tools such as a handgun, TASER, OC spray and baton.

I also conducted several tests in the mat room to determine both the GLOVE's durability and if the GLOVE could be incorporated into various defensive tactics scenarios and handcuffing situations.

In addition to these tests, I have instructed user courses and brought the GLOVE to several defensive tactics training events throughout the Midwest over the past several months. During this time, I have applied the GLOVE to approximately 60 individuals.

Testing of the GLOVE involved multiple trips to the range and the mat room. (Photo/Tyson Kilbey)

During my review and analysis of the GLOVE, I identified several pros and cons. These are initial assessments due to the short period of the time the GLOVE has been available and with the knowledge that pros and cons have a certain level of subjectivity based on the totality of the circumstances of individual incidents.

Pros of the GLOVE

The GLOVE provides pain compliance and a distraction to the peripheral nervous system. There is a variance in its effect between individuals, with some individuals seemingly only mildly affected; however, the substantial majority of individuals were affected during the stimulation phase.

The GLOVE allows for an easy transition to any other tool.

Training and operating costs of the GLOVE are low.

The GLOVE can be used and operated as a pair, or a single GLOVE can be used independently (two officers can each have a GLOVE).

Weapon retention is easily achievable with the GLOVE, as it would be more difficult for someone to take the GLOVE than another tool.

There were no signature marks, redness, or any other signs of physical injury to any of the subjects.

The GLOVE has undergone medical studies to check for safety and efficacy, the results of which have been published by the Institute of Electrical and Electronics Engineers (IEEE).

With the GLOVE, only the area contacted is affected, and therefore it is unlikely that a backing or secondary officer would be adversely affected by the GLOVE.

The GLOVE has an unassuming appearance.

An officer who used the GLOVE in an actual combative situation said that the "GLOVE got the subject to comply quicker than if I did not have it available to me."

CONS of the GLOVE

The GLOVE must be applied in close proximity to the subject.

The GLOVE is a force multiplier; however, officers still require good defensive tactics skills. It would be a mistake for officers to become over-reliant on the GLOVE.

When water is part of the equation, there is a concern when using CEWs.

Because the GLOVE is worn by the officer, there is a chance of inadvertent exposure to the subject if the officer does not realize the GLOVE is in on mode.

Because direct skin contact is required, the GLOVE would not be ideal in situations where the subject is wearing heavy clothing and long sleeves.

The GLOVE was recently named an Innovative Product of the Year for 2019 at the Global Security Exchange (GSX) Conference. Information regarding training, pricing and GLOVE specifications is available at www.complianttechnologies.net.

This chapter examined a variety of self-defense tools that people like to carry and often have questions about in terms of their reliability and effectiveness in self-defense scenarios. While this was by no means and all-encompassing study of these tools I think you now have the framework in place to conduct your own research and testing to see if any of them are the right fit for you. Ultimately, any tool may have value in assisting in self-defense and you the user, is really the most important factor to its success. Are you willing to train with it? How familiar are you with its functions? If the tool requires the use of fine motor skills such as the pressing of a button or squeezing of a trigger, are you willing to develop this skill to a level that you can do it under extreme stress?

Before I close this chapter on defensive tools, I want to make one other important point. "Defensive tool" is only correctly named if that tool is used in defense. Any one of these tools can be more correctly described as offensive tools. For a complete self-defense strategy, some thought, mental rehearsal, and even physical training should be invested in defending against these tools in case they are ever illegally used against you. It would be particularly important to learn and understand the defenses to a tool that you plan to carry. First for the defensive aspect, but also because it will undoubtedly improve your ability to use it effectively by learning its weaknesses. On a final note of caution, it is imperative that you become knowledgeable about legalities involved in your particular tool of choice. Jurisdictions across the country vary considerably on what type of potential weapons are allowed and where, and this information is a must have if you choose to carry a self-defense tool.

You may have noticed that in this chapter I did not discuss the most common self-defense tool in contemporary history; the handgun. Although my first book was dedicated solely to its use, the next chapter will be entirely devoted to firearms for self-defense.

Chapter 4 Most Important Concepts

- There are a variety of defensive tools that are available to carry
- Each tool has an associated list of pros and cons
- Training with your tool of choice is imperative
- Weapons of opportunity exist in most environments
- Learning how to defend against offensive tools should be part of your personal defense strategy
- It is important to know the legalities of defensive tools.

Chapter 5 - Firearms

"A well regulated Militia, being necessary to the security of a free State, the right of the people to keep and bear Arms, shall not be infringed." - The Second Amendment of the United States Constitution

As I may have mentioned once or twice during this book, my first book which was released in April of 2018, was entirely devoted to handguns. I know that many people reading this book have either read or plan to read *Fundamental Handgun Mastery*. Of course, as an author, it is always rewarding to hear feedback from readers regarding what they learned from the book, how they have applied the information into their training philosophies, and how they would like to continue to learn more about the topic.

After twenty years in law enforcement, and over ten years as a firearms instructor for civilians and law enforcement, the study, training, and teaching of firearms has been a major part of my life. I have trained with every level of shooter from absolute beginner to multi-discipline world champions and everything in between. As I continue to teach firearms almost daily, I am still convinced that skill in firearms is based on a strong foundation of two things: Impeccable firearms safety and a deep mental and physical understanding of the fundamentals of marksmanship. There is no magic potion, no mystical bullet fairy, and no special gun modifications that can replace safety and fundamentals.

The four cardinal rules of firearms safety are:

Treat all guns as if they are loaded.

Do not point your gun at anything you are unwilling to shoot.

Keep your finger off the trigger until you are ready to fire.

Be aware of your target, backstop, and beyond.

These four rules provide the structure through which all firearms training I do is built upon. They are universal, and they apply at all times, whether I am shooting or not. The four cardinal rules are designed for combat, for competition, for shooting as a hobby, and for any other fathomable capacity in which a firearm may be included.

As I always tell my students, it is not enough to recite these rules at the beginning of a training session or competition. These rules should be studied, applied, and constantly monitored to ensure adherence to at all times. When I explain these rules to new shooters or review them for experienced shooters, I often attach stories I have been told through the years that illustrate what happens when one or more of these rules is violated. It is one thing to hear someone say, "Treat all guns as if they are loaded." But it has an entirely different impact to say, "The gun owner who thought the gun that he left in the garage was unloaded, will never again see his three-year-old daughter who found it while playing." In my opinion, there should be a visceral and oftentimes somber moment in every safety discussion about firearms. The point must constantly be re-enforced that gun safety requires constant, meticulous focus and attention. Anything less than that is completely unacceptable.

Teaching gun safety to children is another passion of mine. Parents ask me all the time, "What age is appropriate to teach gun safety to children?" My answer has always been and remains to this day: as soon as possible. Teaching kids exactly what to do if they ever come across an unsecured gun in any environment is never a bad thing. This is what I teach:

Stop.

Do not touch.

Leave the area.

Tell a trusted adult.

As far as teaching children the actual fundamentals of marksmanship and the handling and shooting of firearms, that is generally a case by case basis, but with low recoil guns like 22 caliber rifles, this can be done fairly easily under the direction of a qualified instructor at an early age. Teaching children unwavering respect for firearms safety is one of the more important things gun owners can do to provide for a future of responsible gun ownership. In the area of firearms safety, we all have a responsibility to do our part.

Once a foundation of safety is firmly established, the next step is to learn and constantly improve on the fundamentals of marksmanship. These are the seven fundamentals: grip, stance, sight picture, sight alignment, trigger control, breathing, and follow-through.

The principles of a good grip are solid contact between the shooter's hands and the gun, the web of the shooting hand placed high on the back of the gun to help control the recoil and firm pressure on both sides of the gun. In many respects, the grip is unique to the shooter and is something that should be practiced and experimented with on an individual basis with the assistance of a qualified instructor.

A shooter's stance is also somewhat unique to the individual. In general terms, the stance is what provides the platform by which to shoot from. With this in mind, knees bent, weight slightly forward toward the balls of the feet, and feet situated approximately shoulder-width apart are key components to a good stance. The ultimate goal is to provide a balanced and stable platform, but also to be capable of movement if the need were to arise.

Sight picture involves what the shooter sees. For marksmanship shooting, the shooter should generally be looking at three different distances. The rear sights located on the back of the gun, the front sight located toward the front of the gun, and the target at whatever distance it is located from the shooter. For precise, accurate shots with a handgun, most shooters need to focus on the front sight (specifically the top edge of the front sight) while merely seeing the target and rear sights. This is accomplished by looking through the gun towards the intended target. For most guns, the front sight should be placed directly in the middle of the target. For close-quarter combat shooting, it is acceptable to look at the target while merely seeing the sights briefly as they are raised up to meet the threat. This is sometimes referred to as "flash sight picture" and is done in cases when the threat is in close proximity and time is of the essence.

Sight alignment is the procedure by which you properly aim a semi-automatic pistol. Essentially, the rear sights and front sight should be aligned in a manner that the front sight is at the exact same height as the rear sights. If this happens when the shot is fired, the shot should not land higher or lower than where the shooter intends. Furthermore, the front sight should be oriented exactly in the middle of the rear sights. Any error to the left or right of the intended target is an indication that the front sight was either too far left or too far right when the shot was fired; as opposed to exactly in the middle of the rear sights. Essentially, as a very basic rule, where the front sight is located when the shot is fired is the direction in which the bullet will go.

Trigger control is the process by which the shooter uses their trigger finger to initiate the shot. It is important to press the trigger in a smooth motion by applying constant pressure until the shot breaks. Any unintended or additional movement in the gun during this process can cause the shot to land off the target.

Trigger control requires consistent, focused practice and is a perishable skill.

Focused breathing, as addressed earlier in this book, is helpful in so many areas of physical performance. Shooting is no different. In addition to allowing you to clearly focus on the other fundamentals without creating additional fatigue, the moment you completely exhale is often referred to as your "natural respiratory pause" and is an excellent time to break your shot as this will likely be a time of minimal movement in your overall shooting platform.

Finally, the concept of follow-through is completing the process of shooting back to your holster. Once you shoot, you should be resetting your shooting position as efficiently as possible to prepare for a follow-up shot. Once you are sure a follow-up shot is unnecessary, a good practice is to take your finger off the trigger, scan the environment around you, and return your gun to its holster in the exact reverse order you used to draw it.

I wanted to share with you two articles I have written in the two-year span between *Fundamental Handgun Mastery* and *Personal Defense Mastery*. The first one appeared in PoliceOne in August of 2018, and the second one appeared in American Shooting Journal in September of 2018. These articles illustrate some of the principles and philosophies I have shared so far in this book, as well as with students through the years.

5 underused ways to improve police firearms training

(Featured in PoliceOne August 12th, 2018)

Cops often complain that firearms training is boring, static and geared strictly toward the passing of a state-mandated qualification course – but it doesn't have to be that way

Firearms training is an essential component of any agency's subject control program. As I train with law enforcement officers across the country, one common complaint I hear is that firearms training is boring, static and geared strictly toward the passing of a state-mandated qualification course. As a result, many officers don't see their range time as an opportunity to polish a life-saving skill, but rather a necessary evil to satisfy the brass. Worse yet, many officers are not motivated to train with their handgun or develop their skill level past what they are taught in the police academy.

This article is a reminder that there are some underused ways to add excitement and value to your firearms training regimen. All of them are relatively easy to implement, and I can attest that they have greatly enhanced my current firearms training programs.

The two most important things to consider with any firearms training are safety and the fundamentals of marksmanship. With that in mind, I try to regularly incorporate the following five concepts and drills into training:

1. Video review and breakdown

With the ease in which videos can be taken, there is no good reason not to use this technology as a training tool! Record range drills and allow students to conduct a self-assessment and debrief session with instructors. When students get to watch themselves perform drills such as reloads, lateral movement, follow-up shots, or malfunction clearances on camera, they can pick up on wasted movements and other inefficiencies they may not even realize they are doing. With this recognition of the problem, performance improvement comes at a substantially faster rate.

2. Shooting competition

Law enforcement officers tend to be competitive. One way to reignite and motivate officers to perform at a higher level is to introduce an in-house competition. There are a number of ways to do this in a safe, fun and cost-efficient manner.

One simple way is to run a cumulative score of a paper qualification, a timed steel plate or bowling pin course, and a timed obstacle course that incorporates a couple of shooting positions and obstacles to shoot around such as wooden barricades, barrels, or mailboxes. As with any competition, rewards such as medals, ribbons and gift-certificates should be given to the winner (or top three to five shooters) depending on the size of the department.

As a way to motivate all skill levels, run the competition annually or even bi-annually with additional awards given to the officers who demonstrate the most improvement over time.

3. Malfunction and communication drill with a partner

One drill I have successfully used is conducted in the following way. Two shooters line up and make their weapons ready. Then both of them hand me their magazines. While they face downrange, I place dummy rounds in one or both of their magazines and hand them back to them. I then call the various strings of fire. The shooters are responsible for both clearing the malfunction caused by the dummy round and communicating with their partner that they need cover as they clear the malfunction. Not only do they get to polish the fundamentals, they get to perform under the stress caused by malfunctions and successfully communicate with a partner under those conditions. This is a great drill to work on tactics and an outstanding drill to incorporate video review into as well.

4. Follow-through drill

Most range drills end with a final shot then scan and recover to the holster. It is a good idea to go beyond the re-holstering process and include additional follow-up procedures into your drills. For example, have the officers give radio transmissions of locations and suspect descriptions while moving to a position of cover. Not only does this require safe and thoughtful action, it translates well to proper tactics in the real world.

5. Alternative starting positions

The overwhelming majority of range drills begin with officer's hands in the interview position or down at their sides; but not all deadly force encounters happen when an officer's hands are in this position. It is a good idea to start strings of fire under different circumstances. For example, some strings of fire should be started while the officer is holding pepper spray or a TASER, requiring the officer to transition to the handgun on the command of fire. Another option is to have the officer hold a notebook or clipboard prior to the command of fire, or have an officer begin the string of fire from a seated position.

Conclusion

Safety and the fundamentals of marksmanship are the two primary components of any good firearms program. Once those two elements are in place, it is incumbent on firearms trainers to develop realistic, challenging and productive range drills for their agency. By doing this, officers will be motivated to increase their skill and proficiency levels, and everyone will benefit. Train hard and be safe!

****

A.T.O.M.S. -Five Essential Components of Concealed Carry

(Featured in American Shooting Journal September 2018 Issue)

I have had the incredible opportunity to teach nearly a thousand students in my concealed carry classes over the last six years. The experience levels of my students have ranged from lifelong gun owners to people who have never fired a gun prior to my course. I have been consistently honored to teach students who have willingly given up their time and money to learn about an incredibly important topic that may one day save an innocent life!

In this article, I want to share some of the most important concepts and strategies I have learned to take your concealed carry to the highest, safest, and most efficient level possible. I have fit this strategy into the acronym A.T.O.M.S. so that you can easily remember it. Atoms are often referred to as the building blocks of all matter. In the following article, I will layout the most essential building blocks of an effective concealed carry strategy.

Awareness- It is not uncommon to hear people say things like "awareness is key" and "situational awareness could have saved them." But what exactly does that mean? When it comes to you and your family's personal safety, it means a lot of things. Do you have a visual of the people around you? If you are indoors, do you know where the primary and secondary entrances and exits are? Are there additional exits such as windows that could be used in the case of an extreme emergency (i.e. Active Shooter)? Are there places that can be used as cover or concealment in the case of a shooting? These are quick, easy, questions you can ask yourself when you are out in public whether or not you are carrying concealed. But this is only the tip of the iceberg in terms of being keenly aware of the things going on around you. If you do it enough, it becomes habit forming and part of how you observe the world. By doing this, you could possibly avert danger before it even happens. This would be the best case scenario!

Training – For concealed carry citizens, the importance of training cannot be overstated. Can you be too good, too accurate, or too well trained for a gun fight that may save your life? So what are some of the most effective training strategies? First, dry fire draws from your concealed carry holster is a must! This means making one hundred percent certain that your gun is unloaded, then practicing drawing the gun from your concealed carry holster. This is only costs you time, and is an incredibly effective way to build positive repetitions. A few draws a week translates into dozens of draws a month, and hundreds of extra draws a year!

In live fire training, many people "warm up" by shooting slow speed fundamental drills. While these are great, I would suggest that during some of your training sessions, you start off with faster, more dynamic shooting from your concealed carry holster. The premise behind this concept is that nearly every self-defense shooting happens when you are "cold" not after you have had the chance to warm up. The only time you can mimic this is at the very beginning of your training session. Try shooting a threat target at the very beginning of your next shooting session. The only acceptable outcome is a one hundred percent hit rate as quickly and efficiently as you are capable of accomplishing.

Overall Strategy – Carrying Concealed is only a small portion of your overall personal defense strategy. Not all self-defense situations call for the use of a firearm. In addition to carrying concealed and practicing with your gun, you should also take every opportunity you can to learn and practice empty hand self-defense (my preferred style is Gracie Jiu-Jitsu). You should also invest some time in learning about the various less than lethal tools (pepper spray, stun guns) available to you for those times and situations where carrying you firearm is not feasible. Finally, an overall strategy must include taking legal classes and seminars so that you are familiar with the laws in your state.

Mental Rehearsal – While physically training with your gun and in various self-defense arts is important, I would suggest that mental training is equally important. Putting yourself in various self-defense scenarios in the most common places you are at will undoubtedly prepare you to act more effectively in the case of an emergency. By rehearsing your escape route, or your move to a position of cover, or even your angle in which you would launch and effective counter-attack to a threat, you are giving yourself a plan of action so you won't have to come up with it during a moment of high stress where making those types of decisions won't be near as easy, or even possible at all!

Safety – Concealed Carry citizens have no choice but to put safety at the highest level possible. For all of us, that is the correct thing to do. Throughout the years, I have asked my students to be an example of firearms safety wherever they go and every time they shoot. Muzzle discipline, trigger finger discipline, awareness of your target and surroundings, and the treatment of all guns with the respect a loaded firearm deserves are the basic tenants of firearm safety that make up any effective firearm strategy.

Carrying concealed is a valuable right, and a tremendous responsibility. By building your concealed carry strategies on A.T.O.M.S. I have no doubt that you will become very successful in your training and preparation. This is a win for the good guys. Train hard, be safe, and see you on the range!

****

I wanted to re-iterate the primary reason I have chosen to share so many of the articles I have written in this book. As I have said previously, I hope that by now you have identified some recurring themes amongst all chapters. These are pillars of my overall personal defense strategies that can be applied to most situations. By recognizing these themes, you will have the tools and concepts necessary to build your own personal defense strategies.

There is so much to share about firearms and training, but I specifically would like to focus on two final concepts related to firearms before closing. Then I will close the chapter with some of my favorite drills for you to try at the range.

First, I want to discuss the value of weapon retention and why you should incorporate it into your training. Then I want to discuss the process of dry firing and why it should also be included in your firearms training.

Weapon retention is the concept of ensuring that your firearm is completely under your control. This concept can extend to the safe storage of all of your firearms, and absolutely should. But for now, I want to focus on weapon retention when you are carrying concealed. First, a quality holster or purse/bag in which you carry your weapon in is essential. If the holster you have chosen does not securely maintain your weapon, then choose another one. Also, if you choose purse carry, make sure that there is a specific portion of the purse designated to secure your weapon. Next, always consider your position relative to others in terms of weapon retention. If someone is within six to eight feet of you, they are at distance to attempt to forcibly take your weapon from you in a short amount of time. Knowing this and having a plan to fight off this type of attack is crucial. Pay particular attention to someone who appears to be glancing at the location on your body where your weapon is holstered. This is a possible pre-attack indicator. Finally, understand that when someone is actively attempting to take your weapon from you this is a serious situation. You need a reliable course of action and there is zero room for hesitation.

I want to reiterate what is undoubtedly one of the most essential components of firearms skill development: dry firing. Dry firing is the practice of drawing, manipulating, and practicing with your gun without the use of live ammunition. You can practice virtually every single fundamental of marksmanship while dry firing and act in accordance with the four rules of firearms safety at all times when dry firing your handgun. Furthermore, you can practice a smooth efficient draw, clearing common malfunctions, and performing reloads. All of these skills make up a complete firearms training regimen. Find a safe location, make certain that no live ammunition is anywhere near you, and practice! If there is a secret to excellence in firearms, dry firing your pistol is the secret.

I know many of you reading this practice shooting with your handguns. Unfortunately, many people go to the firing range but have no idea what kind of drills to practice or how to gauge improvement. So, I want to share with you some ideas in that area. During the course of your training, you should run drills that involve you drawing your weapon and putting at least one positive hit on target in the quickest amount of time possible. Also, you should practice strings of

113

fire that require you to successfully hit multiple targets. If you are shooting with a partner, have them call out shoot and no-shoot targets, to help practice shooting, target recognition, and decision making at the same time. Practice drills that require reloads to complete. For example, establish two targets, then load your gun with only one round. This will force you to reload to complete the drill. Finally make sure practice shooting at varying distances, using only one hand, and in various lighting conditions. If you are safe and understand the fundamentals, you are only limited by your creativity. For more drills and ideas, follow Top Firearms Instruction on YouTube and Facebook.

In the next chapter, I will share with you a wide variety of personal defense topics. Each one deserves further exploration and consideration as you move forward in developing your overall personal safety plan.

Chapter 5 Most Important Concepts

> There are four rules of firearms safety that you must commit to memory as part of your firearms training

- Teaching others, including children, is one of the responsibilities of gun owners
- There are seven fundamentals of marksmanship that are the foundation of all shooting from beginner to advanced
- Armed the safety and fundamentals, use your imagination to keep your training fun, realistic, and efficient, as described in the articles in this chapter
- Weapon retention is an important topic and should be part of your personal defense strategy
- Dry firing your weapon is one of the most important things you can do to further your skill development.
- If you understand firearms safety and know the fundamentals of marksmanship, you are only limited by your creativity

Chapter 6 - Personal Defense Extras

__Though violence is not lawful, when it is offered in self-defense or for the defense of the defenseless, it is an act of bravery far better than cowardly submission. The latter befits neither man nor woman. Under violence, there are many stages and varieties of bravery. Every man must judge this for himself. No other person can or has the right.__ –Mahatma Gandhi

This chapter will be comprised of a collection of personal defense topics and principles. Each of these topics could warrant an entire chapter (or even book) in their own right; however, meaningful information can be obtained by understanding the basics of each concept. Furthermore, since the overriding theme of this book has been the connection in principles across every facet of personal defense, you should be developing the framework necessary to develop defense strategies regardless of the specific topic. This chapter can be summed up as a fast-paced glimpse into the voluminous world of personal defense related categories. My intention is for you to recognize this and explore them in more detail. Not only will this better prepare you, but it will serve to keep things interesting and add variety to your training. Also, when you are faced with a scenario you have not dealt with, it can be thought-provoking in addition to an enhancement to your current understanding of your knowledge and skills.

The topics I will cover in this chapter are the following: Verbal De-escalation, Physical Health and Diet, First Aid, Response to the Active Shooter, Domestic Violence, Workplace Safety, Home Defense, Church Safety, Terrorism, Traveling, Carjacking, Sexual Assault and Date Rape, Legal Considerations, Internet Safety, Ambush Prevention, and Teaching Family, Friends and Children.

Verbal De-escalation

De-escalation is a fascinating topic for several reasons. First, because it is often misunderstood. Second, many people are under the impression that it is an ability you are either born with or not. There is no doubt that some people have a pre-disposed inclination to effective communication. As you read this you can probably picture people you know who fall into this category. For those that do not have this gift, all is not lost. In my experience, the ability to use verbal skills to successfully de-escalate a tense situation can be substantially improved. There are many quality books and training courses dedicated to this exact topic.

The reason I suggest that de-escalation is misunderstood is because many people are under the impression that de-escalation means saying anything necessary to completely avoid all conflict. If that was the case then in every situation you could just give up your ground until the aggressor is happy and gets what they want. This is counterproductive because this puts you at the complete discretion of the attacker. Furthermore, it only increases your likelihood of becoming a victim on a reoccurring basis. In certain cases that have escalated beyond control, the best immediate decision may be to verbally comply with an aggressor until you can regain a position of advantage. For example, if a mugger is pointing a gun at you asking for your wallet or purse, that would be a time to verbally comply. This is provided that it is clear that property or money is all the aggressor is after.

Skillful de-escalation is the ability to verbally diffuse situations before they become an incident involving physical force. If a physical incident can be avoided, most often that is the best option. De-escalation is a valuable skill for first responders as well as civilians. For the remainder of this section, I will highlight the most essential components of de-escalation I have learned over the years.

First, do not take verbal "attacks" personally. Instead, attempt to decipher the emotion behind the attack. This will often reveal what the person arguing with you is actually upset about. Next, do not sacrifice your physical safety in an attempt to verbally appease an aggressor. Make sure that you are constantly placing yourself in a position to react physically if the need were to arise. This would include maintaining the appropriate distance and placing physical barriers between you and the subject. It also includes using the tactics I described in an early chapter of creating the appropriate distance and angle while speaking with your hands up and in front of you. Putting the problem in terms of "we" can make it seem as if you are working as a team as opposed to against each other. "What can we do to solve this?" "Let's work through this." These the type of phrases that have the best odds of eliciting a positive response. Finally, learn to consciously detect standoffs in which neither side is budging. When this happens, you have to recognize it and have the adaptability to redirect the conversation.

As I mentioned earlier, there is a mountain of information about the skill and art of de-escalation. Through the years I have attended numerous courses and read several books devoted entirely to this topic. It is a valuable skill that in the right incident, could have life-saving implications. I have witnessed police officers avert possible tragic consequences through articulate interpersonal communication skills. If you are serious about personal defense, it is a skill worth developing.

Physical Health and Diet

There is no doubt that physical health is an essential part of a personal defense strategy. Without being physically healthy, it would be difficult if not impossible to train in an effective way to protect yourself and your loved ones. This seems obvious, but I cannot count how many times I have seen and spoken with people in the gun world who claim to practice for "self-defense" but do not do anything to maintain their physical health. The truth is, I would actually start a personal defense program with health as the first essential pillar of its foundation. When it comes to physical health, while working out is no doubt important, I would suggest diet is more important. I realize that at the time of this writing we are inundated with information on fitness and diet. I do not have the time in this book to address it but I cannot emphasize this enough. Make your physical health a priority through some form of exercise and a healthy diet. "But it costs too much to eat a healthy diet!" Well, as the saying goes, "It costs a lot more to be sick." Do not fall into the excuse trap of not having enough time. We all have the same amount of hours in a day, and your physical health demands some of that time!

First Aid

First aid is yet another area that until recently was often overlooked in terms of a personal defense strategy. But, in the aftermath of mass shootings and other tragedies involving extreme physical injury: automobile collisions, attacks with guns, knives, or other weapons, etc. it has become clear that knowledge of basic first aid and casualty care is essential. At a bare minimum, you should familiar and proficient with the basic CPR steps, how to use an Automated External Defibrillator (AED), how to handle choking and airway obstruction (abdominal thrusts), how and when to apply a tourniquet, and what to do in case of bleeding from the head, chest, or neck area (pressure and bandaging). Many entities provide this type of training, and this should be part of your overall plan. It should be self-explanatory the life-saving implications these skills have and why they are necessary for personal safety.

Response to the Active Shooter

For this section, I want to share one of the posts from my Training Tip of Day Blog regarding this subject. I wrote this tip after one of the major incidents in the national news.

***Training Tip of the Day Active Shooter Response**-I do not care if you are pro-gun or anti-gun, democrat or republican, Red Sox or Yankees fan, DEVELOP A PLAN for Active Shooter Incidents. In this post I am going to give you a start with the MOST ESSENTIAL elements of an effective response. There are three proven responses, each one is an option, and you determine at the moment which is most appropriate. Response number one---GET OUT and AWAY! Leave anything non-essential and get as far away as possible from danger. Do not think conventionally, if a door is not an option for escape, then breaking through a window with a chair might be an option. Your mission is to escape. Make it happen. Do not give the killer targets. Response number two--- BARRICADE in place and LOCK the shooter out! Do NOT just "hide." Lock the door. Put chairs, desks, any heavy objects you can locate against the door. Make penetrating the area you are in a difficult if not impossible task. Your mission is to become inaccessible to the shooter. Response number three---OVERWHELM the Shooter and STOP the*

THREAT! Trying to shoot people while being attacked is a difficult task. If the shooter is already in your immediate presence it is time for EVERYONE who is willing to throw bags, purses, chairs, any objects at the shooter. It is time to use the fire extinguisher on the shooter. It is time to OVERWHELM the killer in such a way that it is impossible for them to shoot at defenseless victims. There is more to it than this, but these are the essentials that you must begin thinking about and reviewing in both your personal and professional life now!

Response to the active shooter has been an important area of focus for the last couple of decades. These horrific incidents are the reason that many law enforcement officers and trained civilians carry in churches, restaurants, and a variety of other public locations. Response to the active shooter is a multi-faceted subject which includes acute awareness, analysis of the location to determine how "soft" a target it is, locating escape routes, positions of immediate barricade and cover, all weapons of improvisation, and knowledge of basic first aid.

Domestic Violence

Unfortunately, domestic violence remains one of the most deadly and real threats anyone can face. The complication of emotional and personal factors involved in domestic situations does nothing to help the matter. There is no coincidence that when someone is murdered the spouse, boyfriend, girlfriend, or significant other is always the first person of interest in solving the crime.

As a law enforcement officer, I have responded to many calls involving domestic violence. By the time the situation has escalated to the point in which police intervention is required, emotions from both sides are usually too high to effectively work toward a resolution at that moment. Some of the common themes in domestic violence situations are the abuse of drugs and alcohol, and emotional abuse by the attacker long before and up to the point of physical abuse.

There is no easy answer to this problem. Recognizing the signs as early as possible and making the difficult but important decision to remove yourself from a domestic violence situation is critical for your safety. If you feel as though you are being manipulated you probably are. If you find yourself making excuses for their inappropriate behavior you probably are. The problem is not with you, and it is not your fault.

Unfortunately, it is up to you to solve it. There are several resources available for victims of domestic violence and local law enforcement and advocacy groups exist to help direct victims to these resources.

Workplace Safety

With the knowledge that a substantial portion of the average person's day and week is spent at their place of employment, it stands to reason that part of a personal safety plan includes what to do in case of an emergency at work. Employers should take an active role in this through policies, procedures, and training in areas such as evacuations, emergency staging areas, intruder drills, and overall site security. If the employer does not, it is up to the employee to bring this topic to the forefront. The best-case scenario is an engaged, working relationship between employers and employees working together to maximize workplace safety. Workplace violence is, unfortunately, something that has become all too common in American culture.

Home Defense

Principles of Home Defense has become one of my favorite training courses to teach over the years. Whether it is in the format of a group of neighbors, or a personal session with one specific family, it is always rewarding to assist and watch as they build defense systems for their most valued place of safety-their homes.

The fundamental principles of home defense include locking mechanisms at all entry points, safely secured weapons in the home, and mentally and physically rehearsing emergency plans. One drill I do with students is to ask them to play the role of "bad guy" in terms of invading or burglarizing their homes. This shift in perspective is oftentimes extremely eye-opening in terms of where home security weaknesses exist.

Some of the best ways to strengthen your home defense included alarm systems, signs for alarms, cameras, dogs, and teaming up with neighbors to provide additional watchful eyes. A combination of these things might be the best overall strategy for home defense. Furthermore, consistently evaluating and updating your home defense plan is ideal.

Church Safety

In a perfect world, a place of worship would be exempt from acts of violence. Unfortunately, several times throughout the last two decades, churches have been the scene of horrendous acts of violence and mass murder. Acts of terrible violence such as these shock the conscience of society, but they have been repeated over and over again. There is probably not one single answer to the problem, although there is certainly something that can be done immediately. Churches have to refuse to be soft targets. It is not the church leadership's fault that these events occur; however, it is certainly up to those responsible for the church to enact safety measures to protect their congregation.

Throughout the years it has been my privilege to work with pastors and church security teams to enhance their safety measures. It is important to address ongoing training and re-evaluation of your church's security procedures. There has been a recent trend in churches being pro-active in increasing their security through armed teams, cameras, and ongoing training. If this is not happening at your church right now, make it a priority to talk to the church leadership to address the issue.

Terrorism

In modern history, no event has been more impactful in terms of awakening the American populace to the reality of terrorist attacks than the events that occurred on September 11th, 2001. There had certainly been attacks before, and there have been attacks since, in all areas of the world. In this era, the possibility of terrorist attacks certainly deserves to be addressed in terms of a personal safety plan.

There is an extremely broad definition of what a terrorist attack truly is and how an attack can be carried out. A terrorist attack can be carried out in the form of shooting, bombing, using vehicles as weapons, and more. The goal is oftentimes to make a statement by attacking the civilian population and claiming a large number of victims. The same principles of situational awareness discussed in this book can be used to recognize and potentially interrupt an attack. Understanding what a soft target is, especially when a large number of people are gathered together is imperative. Furthermore, trusting your instincts when something or someone does not seem right is critical.

Traveling

Traveling is another topic of concern when it comes to personal safety. The difficulty with traveling, especially when you are at a location for the first time, is the complete lack of "home-field advantage." It can be a challenge to know which areas pose the greatest risk, and it can also be difficult not to stand out as a tourist. Unfortunately, this fact alone can increase your chances of being viewed as a target. Along with the strategies discussed in this book, keeping plans confidential from strangers as well as conducting preliminary research before traveling is essential. Also, reaching out to people who know the area and checking travel advisories is important pre-travel research.

Carjacking

The term carjacking as most people understand it refers to a typically egregious form of robbery in which an automobile is stolen by force. In some parts of the world, this crime is more prevalent than others, but it certainly can be a dangerous, life-changing situation. Knowing your location, applying the strategies of defensive driving from Chapter 2, and keeping your doors secure are all steps in the right direction. In the defensive driving chapter, I listed several advantages to leaving at least one length of vehicle space between your car and the one directly in front. If nothing else, having an escape route through rapid acceleration away from the attack might very well be the most effective course of action.

Sexual Assault and Date Rape

This brutal and manipulative crime is something that must be addressed in modern times. It can be complicated for a range of reasons to include the use of alcohol or other drugs, the stigma and embarrassment which is often associated with it, and the physical and emotional trauma that accompanies it. To further complicate the matter, the victim may be even more discouraged when their side of the story is not believed due to the popularity or convincing demeanor of the perpetrator. Both women and men need to address this issue in full force in the years to come and take every reasonable measure to teach everyone the best strategies to recognize, prevent, and stop in the act this particularly heinous crime from occurring.

Legal Considerations

One thing many people do not think about, or adequately prepare for, is the aftermath of a self-defense situation. After being involved in an incident, particularly one in which a weapon of some sort was used and injury or death occurred, you can count on years of legal battles in the aftermath. This is where having an action plan is critical. The last thing you want is to have to do the research necessary to find a qualified attorney once the incident occurred. Legal issues are an area where many people give advice, but few are qualified to do so. I am not a lawyer and do not claim to be one. So my advice to you is to research businesses and organizations that provide this service and develop an after-action strategy just in case.

Internet Safety

In modern times, a safety plan cannot be considered complete without some focus on internet safety. This ranges from teaching your kids about internet dangers to understanding the insane amount of information that can be gathered about you online. Far too many people underestimate the amount of information criminals can obtain about you before stealing from you, or even worse causing you or your family physical harm. First, I suggest restricting any apps that make your location accessible to the general public. Then I would highly scrutinize all the information you have public on social media. One of my rules is if you do not want even your worst enemy to know about it, do not post it online. I would highly recommend attending a social media course with content on how much information can be obtained online. Most people I know who have attended a course of this type have been amazed by how much information they thought was private was actually readily available.

Ambush Prevention

One of the more horrifying and difficult types of attacks to defend against is the ambush. This is a broad term that can be applied to a police officer responding to a call for service or civilian in everyday life just going from one place to another. Whether carried out by a terrorist or some other criminal, it could be specifically targeted or the target could be chosen at random. As a general rule, the element of surprise is what gives such a tremendous advantage to the attacker in these situations. Therefore, it is our job to use the strategies discussed in this book to minimize the element of surprise as much as possible. There is likely no way to eliminate it completely, but increasing visual awareness and paying particular attention to areas of vulnerability is an excellent start.

Teaching Family, Friends, and Children

The final "extra" that I wanted to share with you in this chapter is the value of sharing the personal defense strategies you discover with family, friends, and the next generation. I have made a lifestyle out of doing just that, and there are very few things that have been as fulfilling and rewarding as this has been. There is also a tremendous element of self-improvement involved because teaching keeps you sharp. Furthermore, the legacy of passing possibly life-saving knowledge to others is an unmatched and worthwhile experience.

****

This chapter of safety extras was in no way all-encompassing. Because these topics have come up over the years in a variety of classes I wanted to include them here for you to consider in your overall defensive strategies. Human trafficking, School Campus Safety, Jogging and Trail-Way Safety, and Special Location Safety such as movie theaters, concerts, and sports arenas were all potential subsections of this chapter. At the risk of being overly-repetitive, which I am not worried about because of how important it is—apply the concepts of personal safety to any location and encounter you find yourself in! The players and environment might change, but the principles are universal.

In the next chapter, I will share with you some of my philosophies regarding training. Some of them are specific to firearms and self-defense, while others are broader in scope and can be applied to any area of skill development you wish.

Chapter 6 Most Important Concepts

> ➢ This chapter offered a rapid-fire glimpse into various other considerations in terms of overall personal defense. They are meant to guide and encourage you to explore these areas as additional training topics for you to explore. The list is by no means exhaustive but exists primarily as an advertisement into the world of possibilities

Chapter 7 - Training

Live as if you were to die tomorrow. Learn as if you were to live forever. –Mahatma Gandhi

It is so common for students, friends, and training partners of mine from around the world to ask me what I enjoy the most. Is it going to the range and shooting? Is it spending a few hours in the mat room training martial arts? Is it going to the driving course and competing to get my best time? The truth is I genuinely enjoy each of these activities and participate in one or more of them every day.

But if I had to be pinned down to what my favorite thing to do is, the answer would without question be training in a general. I categorize training in a rather broad sense. To me, training means both teaching, and practicing individually (or with a group) the skills you wish to improve upon. Basically, throughout my years in the various fields of study in this book, I have grown to love the process. If there is any secret to how I have been able to succeed as a firearms or martial arts instructor that is it.

I have often heard stories of some of the most successful people in their various fields and it is not uncommon to hear them described as "the first person to show up, and the last person to leave." Almost without question, people who are good at their craft, love what they do.

This is what I think is missing from many people's perspectives when it comes to training. So many people consider training as the necessary evil of skill development. They consider training something that they have to struggle or fight their way through to be good at whatever endeavor they have chosen to embark upon. But I completely disagree with this viewpoint. In the competition world, training is where the championships are won. In the self-defense world, training and preparation are where the critical survival skills that save lives are developed. Success is built and sustained upon the ongoing process of training.

Your training must be adaptable. What I mean is that you have to be willing to train by yourself, with others of either more or less knowledge than you, and at varying times of the day. The reason I think this is so important is that this approach will maximize your training time. Let me apply this to working out at the gym. How many people say, "I need someone to workout with so I have an accountability partner."? The answer is a lot. The problem is what happens when that system does not work and your gym partner quits and your persuasion does not convince them to continue training? Do you quit? Do you find another training partner? I suggest that you discover ways to train with or without a partner. There are benefits to both. But when you can do either one at a moment's notice, then no matter what contingency life throws at you, you will continue to improve.

One extremely common complaint people have about training is that they get bored easily. Think about how many people start a workout or training program only to keep up for a few months (or less) then quit out of boredom. This is completely understandable. It is also exactly why I am constantly searching for ways to mix up my training regiments. Once adding variety becomes an essential part of your training style and curriculum, not only does boredom become less of a factor, but you begin to push yourself out of your comfort zone and tap into your creative abilities. This is critical for skill development.

In this chapter devoted to training, I wanted to share with you some of the most popular and well-engaged training tips of the day I have posted on my blog and social media pages for Top Firearms Instruction in the two years between books. Some of them apply to firearms, while others apply to the self-defense and mindset and other various aspects of personal defense.

137

Many of these tips will re-iterate concepts that have already been discussed, and many will be repeated themes amongst themselves. These were written over an extended period as situations, questions, and suggestions came up among students.

Training Tips of the Day
(Top Firearms Instruction)

➤ Training Tip #1 **Learn like a child**-Have you ever noticed that children acquire new skills at an exponentially faster rate than most adults? Do you ever wonder why this is the case? Over the last decade of training thousands of students, I have an idea. When adults learn, they are bringing quite a bit of previous experience and pre-conceived notions with them. As counterintuitive as that may seem, this oftentimes slows the learning process. Meanwhile, without a lot of previous experience, children tend to be sponges ready to soak in all knowledge about the world around them. They are simply ready to learn. My take away from this is that if adults want to learn something, they should forget about preconceived notions just for a moment, and attempt to learn the skill as a total and complete beginner. I believe anyone who does this will be amazed at the results.

➢ Training Tip #2 **Enjoy Training** -For today's training tip, I thought I would share with you part of my perspective about training. People constantly ask me how I can train so often and so consistently. First and foremost I keep training fun. For ideas on how to accomplish this, stay tuned for future tips or review many tips from the past! Beyond that, I understand that progression and improvement are not achieved in a straight upward line. You will have good days, bad days, and days that are just average. But it is critical to remember that if you are being safe, dry firing your gun, hitting the range, or hitting the mat room, you are WINNING! That is what is important and that is what will keep you improving for life!

➢ Training Tip #3 **Change Things Up**- Although cliché, it is hard to argue that humans are creatures of habit. In terms of skill development, this is not always the best thing. While consistent, focused, repeatable reflexes are ideal in certain segments of the skill-building process, this also leads to plateaus and stagnation. Sometimes this happens without us realizing it. Change things up, practice things you do not think you are good at, and always be open to new drills and ways of doing things. Not only is this fun, but it will also make you better!

➤ Training Tip #4 **Working Through Plateaus**-Training to become proficient in any skill has its ups and downs. Training is also just as much a mental game as it is a physical one. I think it is important to remember that getting better is not always a direct path. You will have good days and bad days as well as what will seem like plateaus in your development. Many people misunderstand this process and subsequently quit because they think they have reached their full potential. On the contrary, pushing past these phases of the learning process is precisely why you will improve. Remember this the next time you have a couple of bad performances at the range. The real battle will be won simply by staying in the game!

➢ Training Tip #5 **Always be a Student-** It is incredible how many "instructors" in both martial arts and firearms only "teach." It appears that these people want the title of instructor before doing the work that the position deserves. This should always raise suspicions amongst current and prospective students. The best teachers are the most dedicated students. If you are a teacher, you owe it to yourself, and more importantly your students, to be just as much a student as you are a teacher. If you are a student who wishes to become a teacher, know that you should and will ALWAYS be a student.

➢ Training Tip #6 **"Adapt what is useful, reject what is useless, and then add what is specifically your own."** - The previous quote is attributed to the legendary Martial Artist, Philosopher, and Actor Bruce Lee. Before I continue writing, I should say I agree with the message. That being said, I think the concept in this quote has been misapplied by a substantial amount of well-intentioned people. Specifically, the "reject what is useless" portion of the quote. In both firearms and empty hand martial arts, I have seen people "reject what is useless" in terms of a technique they are not familiar with, or steps to perform a firearm manipulation, etc. simply because they were not IMMEDIATELY proficient at it. "Yeah, I tried that technique it does not work for me." "I do not do it that way because my hands are too small, my legs are too short," or whatever excuse they come up with. The point I am making is too many people give up on a certain technique or method way before they are qualified to do so. Ultimately, this hurts their skill development and understanding in the long run. So, to end this training tip of the day I give you this quote from an unknown source, "To be good at something, you have to be willing to be bad at it."

➤ Training Tip #7 **Legal Training**-One of the most common deficiencies in the vast majority of citizens' overall self-defense strategy is their basic understanding of the law in regard to self-defense. Throughout the years, I have heard people say, with absolute conviction mind you, statements that have ZERO legal basis. It is not uncommon for people to say, "My brother who is a cop said...or I was reading on a gun debate message board, or I heard that..." Not knowing the law is not a defense, and misunderstanding the law (even with good intentions) is not a defense. Because legal issues are of monumental importance, can be complex, and can change over time, it is critical that you add legal training to your overall program.

➤ Training Tip #8 **Efficiency Filter**- A training concept I use a lot is running what I do through an "efficiency filter." I do not think there is one perfect way to perform a specific handgun function whether it is a reload, a malfunction clear, etc. because external and internal circumstances are fluid in both competition and self-defense situations. I do think that most, if not all of us, can be more efficient in our movements. One of the best ways to discover this is through watching camera footage of your competition stages or range drills. As you conduct these self-assessments, determine where you can be more efficient in your movements, timing, and actions. Doing this will increase your competition times, and overall handgun competency exponentially. In a future training tip, I will discuss segmenting, which is one of the most common mistakes shooters make in terms of efficiency!

➢ Training Tip #9 **Maximizing your Training Sessions-** After an incredible week of training with some of the best in the world at what they do, I thought I would offer a general training tip based on some observations I have made. When you train, be present in the moment. Do not worry about mistakes. Do not question whether or not you are doing every little thing right. Do not set yourself up for failure before you even begin. Instead, look at training as research and experience. I am reminded of the quote, "To be good at something, you have to be willing to be bad at it." The point I'm making is that too many people do not enjoy training get the most they can out of the experience. Learning and skill building is a lifetime journey, enjoy the trip!

➤ Training Tip #10 **Relaxed Versus Tensed Movements-** I was a range officer at a shooting completion recently. The stage I was at included a mandatory reload. One thing I noticed with a lot of shooters that struggled during the reload, was that their movements were extremely tense, they were flexed, jerky, and not smooth in their movements. As a result, several seconds of valuable time was wasted. At a class this past weekend, I took the time to remind the students that SMOOTH IS FAST. Many of us who train hear those words all the time but still resort back to bad habits of tense, rushed movements, especially when time is a concern. Smooth, relaxed movements build solid, repeatable, usable skills. Train hard and be safe friends.

➤ Training Tip #11 **Conservation of Movement and Energy**-To improve efficiency, competition times, tactical exchanges, or any other aspect of your shooting, your primary mission is to find ways to eliminate excessive movement. Excessive movement costs time and energy, both of which are a premium in terms of handgun skills. To determine if your movements can be more direct and concise, it is an excellent idea to video some of your range drills or competition stages and assess where you can be more precise. Furthermore, understand that tense muscles often equate to burning energy unnecessarily. If the movement you are attempting to perform can be done with loose and relaxed muscles, then that is the preferred method. Do a self-assessment during your next range session to see if you can put these two concepts into play to improve your overall performance.

➤ Training Tip #12 **Developing your Draw**- Having a smooth, efficient, and repeatable draw is a major part of your firearms proficiency. Many people neglect this portion of their training, especially if they shoot primarily at indoor ranges where drawing from a holster is sometimes not allowed. The great thing is, the draw can be practiced in a dry setting away from the range. Always make sure to clear and check your weapon and separate any live ammunition from the area before practicing your draw in a dry setting. The mechanics of the draw can be broken down into the following steps: Grip your weapon and release it from the holster **note grip it high on the back strap establishing your shooting grip as soon as you touch it, Lock your wrist and rock toward your target ** note do not fish the gun overhead or bowl the gun in a scooping motion, Put both hands on the gun close to your body, Finally, perfect a smooth and level presentation of the gun toward your target.

➢ Training Tip #13 **Empty Slate-** Today's tip comes from an observation I have made about many adult learners. Adults tend to bring past experiences and preconceived notions into their training sessions, even in topics they have never trained in before. Because of this, they don't learn as much as they could or reach their full potential. The next time you take a class or learn any skill, do your very best to go in with the proverbial "empty slate." Be a kid again, amazed by the world and ready to learn new information! Trust me you will be amazed at how this changes the training experience. All of your prior knowledge will still be there, trust me, but this time you will be surprised at what that slight perspective shift will do for your overall knowledge intake, and subsequently your progress and skill-building

➢ Training Tip #14 **Mental Rehearsal-** While physically training with your gun and in various self-defense arts is important, I would suggest that mental training is equally important. Putting yourself in various self-defense scenarios in the most common places you are at will undoubtedly prepare you to act more effectively in the case of an emergency.

By rehearsing your escape route, or your move to a position of cover, or even your angle in which you would launch an effective counter-attack to a threat, you are giving yourself a plan of action so you will not have to come up with it during a moment of high stress when making those types of decisions will not be near as easy, or even possible at all!

➢ Training Tip #15 **Overreliance on Gear-** Too many shooters look to gun additions and modifications to enhance their shooting. Fancy sights, lasers, grips, trigger modifications, etc. are all nice to have, but they do not make up for consistent, focused practice! When your target does not look quite as good as you want it to, as much as we would like to think it is the gun, it usually is the shooter behind the gun. Invest a little time each week into drawing your gun, working on your grip and stance, seeing sight pictures, and dry firing. This investment will be ten times greater than any additional gear you buy.

➢ Training Tip #16 **Cold Defensive Shooting-** A lot of shooters start their training session with some slow speed fundamental drills. Chances are, if you get into a gunfight, you will not be "warmed up." So working off that premise, the only time you get to practice "cold" so to speak is at the very beginning of your shooting session. So I would suggest that the next couple of shooting sessions you immediately begin by drawing from your concealed carry holster and shooting as quickly as you can accurately hit a threat target. One hundred percent accuracy is your only acceptable outcome and speed and efficiency both matter. Additional concepts to keep in mind is to vary your round count (don't always shoot two rounds), and to consider movement and scanning around the range after each string of fire.

➢ Training Tip #17 **Creative Training Solutions-** One of the lies that we tell ourselves is that we would like to train more but just don't have time. Sometimes we need to be called out on our own lies! Your time is valuable without question, but if you are a gun owner, training is NOT a commodity it is a necessity! So here are some tips I have and still do use to get additional training in when my schedule is packed. 1) When you initially put your handgun on before carrying, take an extra few minutes to do 15 to 20 draws. One week of that and you have done an additional hundred draws as part of a normal routine. 2) Combine segments of training with other activities. For example, I regularly combine dry fire training with my at-home workouts. As another example, an excellent shooter and instructor I know watches television at night while practicing handgun reloads! 3) Put a grip strengthener device in your car or office and during downtime work on your grip strength. These are just a few examples of ways to improve when you are in a time crunch. There are many more and you are only limited by your own creativity.

➢ Training Tip #18 **Cover vs Concealment**-From a tactical and self-defense standpoint, having a firm understanding of the difference between cover and concealment is an essential component to your overall survival strategy.

Concealment is something that makes it more difficult for a threat to see you, but will not necessarily protect from incoming bullets. Examples of concealment might be bushes, drywall, vehicle doors, etc. Cover usually makes it more difficult for a threat to see you AND protects from incoming bullets. Examples of cover might include solid brick walls and vehicle engine blocks. Taking a quick note of cover and concealment locations, especially in locations that you are frequently at, is an excellent part of an overall safety plan.

➢ Training Tip #19 **Physical Fitness-** As if you need even more motivation to get in shape! Shooting is ultimately a physical skill. Whether or not you shoot for competition, hobby, self-defense, or all three. Maintaining your physical fitness level will improve your shooting (among countless other benefits). The body mechanics of grip, stance, shooting platform, shooting from alternative positions and shooting on the move ALL will be improved with an increase in physical fitness. For bonus points, mix your physical workouts in with your dry fire training sessions! Do this for two months and watch your shooting, and overall life, improve substantially!

> Training Tip #20 **Training Mindset-** When it comes to firearms training, I have heard way too many times from people, "I already took that course." Interesting. Did you master all of the information from the course in that one sitting? Analogy. If your child's soccer coach said, "I only have one practice in which I teach the kids to kick then after that we don't practice that anymore." How many games do you think your child's team would win? The point I'm making is that if you want to increase your skill, it is ABSOLUTELY advisable to take additional courses over again. You will be amazed at how much more you can learn and improve by seeing the information again at a different level of experience. I have taken several courses that I enjoy multiple times and have never regretted doing it. Shooting is a

perishable skill that requires attention to detail, focus, and diligent training.

By now I hope you have a clear description of the concepts and overall strategies that I have used over the years to develop personal defense skills. I imagine that some of the concepts resonate well, while others are not your style. This is perfectly normal because we all have to gravitate to the approach that ultimately keeps us training. I am confident the ideas described in this book will give you the foundation to develop your own training methods.

On a final note, one of the reasons I shared with you twenty of my Training Tips of the Day was because I think a few of them will help you in your training endeavors. But beyond that, I want to encourage you to develop your own list of training tips that you learn along the way. I had an absolute blast journaling these tips and they enriched not only my training experiences but also helped me develop as an instructor. I do not doubt that taking a few months to journal your "lessons learned" in your skill development will not only be enjoyable but will help you improve in many of the same ways.

Chapter 7 Most Important Concepts

- ➢ Make your training sessions fun and adaptable
- ➢ This chapter included a myriad of training tips on a variety of topics. Notice the connections between many of the concepts
- ➢ Develop your own strategies to keep engaged with training

Try journaling your own tips and lessons learned along the way

Conclusion

If you love life, don't waste time, for time is what life is made up of. – Bruce Lee

In this book, we have discussed the concepts of personal defense in a variety of contexts. I have shared with you what I have learned through a career in law enforcement, a lifetime of martial arts, and over a decade in the firearms industry. By now you have discovered the overriding themes that are the foundation of personal defense. None the least of which is the knowledge and belief that you are worth defending and you have everything you need to be your best source of defense.

I have shared with you my thoughts on empty-hand self-defense, the most common defensive tools, the handgun, the importance of vehicle safety, mindset and awareness, a handful of extra personal defense categories, and some of my most important training philosophies.

With the information provided to you, I hope that you build your own unique strategies for personal defense that work best for you. Furthermore, I hope that as you discover ideas, techniques, and strategies that yield positive results, you share these lessons with others as part of the process. Most if not all of what I have learned and continue to learn has been through the process of connecting with so many other people of diverse backgrounds, skill levels, and experiences. That has been what has made this so enjoyable.

On a personal note-thank you. Thank you for giving your time to experience this journey with me. I am so honored to have had the opportunity to connect with you so many of you through the years and I do not take for granted the incredible opportunities I have received through the years to spend so much time with people through martial arts, the firearms industry, the law enforcement community, and the private citizens from every imaginable field and background. I plan to continue to teach, as well as learn from many more of you in the days ahead.

With the release of *Personal Defense Mastery,* I will launch new online training tools on my social media accounts. Please follow and subscribe to Top Firearms Instruction on YouTube and Facebook for Training Tips of the Day and the Range Drill of the Week to give you additional ideas on personal training. Also, please leave a review on Amazon of this book so more potential readers can learn and grow from the information!

I wish you luck on your path and I know the process of learning and growing will be both enjoyable and rewarding for you. I know many of you reading this are current or former students and training partners. To those that are not, I hope one day we cross paths in a future class!

Train hard and be safe my friends.

Afterword

Superheroes are often faced with enormous odds. Evil villains, world domination, kryptonite. A brief look at the past few years doesn't seem too different:

2011. September 9th. World Trade Center. 2,977 victims, more than 6,000 injured.

2012. Sandy Hook Elementary. 28 gunned down. 1st graders, teachers.

2017. Las Vegas, Nevada. Music Festival. 58 killed. 413 wounded.

2018. Larry Nassar. 150 women came forward. Sexual assault.

2018. Human trafficking. 50% of the victims are children.

2019. Kansas City. 223 homicides.

Sons. Daughters. Mothers, fathers, brothers, sisters, spouses, friends, strangers. Such violence can make a person feel very small. You may ask yourself: what can *I* do against such violence? Really, what can you do, averaging 137lbs, in the 5-foot range, 60% water?

I remember when I first met Tyson. At the time, I was working in law enforcement and wanted to learn how to better defend myself. Some situations had occurred that made me realize I was an easy target being a small female, so I wanted to remedy that. One of my coworkers told me that Tyson taught jiu-jitsu as well as firearms training. I remember going to that first jiu-jitsu class with apprehension. Before I walked through that door I thought to myself, 'who am I kidding? Who do I think I am, trying to learn jiu-jitsu when I've never trained martial arts or even been in a fight?'

That first class was a pivotal day in my life. After that class, I was on a high. Instead of feeling inferior to defending myself, I realized that I was so much more powerful than I knew. Tyson's understanding of self-defense, his dedication, and most especially his energy were a great experience as a first-timer. Now, three years and a lot of training later, I have my blue belt, am certified in Gracie Jiu-jitsu as a women's self-defense instructor, and have even started my journey in firearms.

When began to read *Personal Defense Mastery*, I thought I would read it over the course of a week. I ended up reading it all in one morning. *Fundamental Handgun Mastery*, Tyson's first book, was a hit, especially for someone like me who had no prior experience with guns. Coupled with his firearms safety class, I had a better foundation for training with firearms than most people ever get (highly recommend both the book and class, especially for beginners)! But when I read the book you are holding in your hands, I couldn't help but think how compelling this book is for those of us faced with that feeling of helplessness: what can we do in the face of violence?

The answer to this violence is personal self-defense. Learning to defend yourself is not simply knowing how to throw a punch. This book covers everything from mindset, verbal de-escalation, martial arts, handgun proficiency, safe driving, first aid, active shooter situations and much more. The fact is, we are all much more powerful than we think. Your mind is more powerful than you think, your body is more powerful than you think. My first class of jiu-jitsu I realized that, and I continue to realize it every time I train. Superheroes aren't born, they're made. It is the ordinary people who train and are mentally prepared that are the champions. In 2015, a train filled with passengers was headed from Amsterdam to Paris. A man began to open fire with an AK47. Anthony Sadler, Alek Skarlatos, and Spencer Stone tackled the gunman.

Spencer Stone used his jiu-jitsu skills to choke the attacker unconscious before anyone was killed. In 2011, Sheila Frederick, a flight attendant, trusted her intuition when she noticed the signs of human trafficking on the plane and was able to rescue a girl. In 2019, Collin Dozier, a wrestler, saved a man who was about to jump off a bridge and commit suicide by pulling him back over the rail in a lock hold. The amazing thing is that once you develop the tools to defend yourself, not only are you a warrior for yourself, but you become a protector of those around you. Whether that's your kids, significant other, friends, or even total strangers, those tools become a protective force for everyone around you. That's what a modern-day superhero looks like.

I've been so grateful to have Tyson as my mentor and cannot tell you how lucky you are to now have his training in book format. This is the time to take personal defense into your own hands. The fact that you are reading this shows that self-defense is important to you. Thankfully, there are people like you who are reading this and want to take that initiative to sharpen your existing skills and gain new ones. You are the true warriors this world needs! In the famous quote of the god Thor: "The answers you seek shall be yours, once I claim what's mine." So claim it. Claim the knowledge, claim the discipline, claim

the training, claim the personal responsibility.
This is your answer to the violence.

-Elizabeth Henderson

About the Author

Tyson Kilbey is a teacher and lifelong student. At the completion of his second book, he has 20 years of law enforcement experience and has worked the ranks of deputy, master deputy, sergeant, and lieutenant. Throughout his career he has worked in detention, patrol, training, SWAT, accident investigation, and has been a member of his agency's competition shooting team. He has a Bachelor of Science in Justice Studies from Fort Hays State University, and has been studying various martial arts for 20 years. He has taught thousands of law enforcement officers across the Midwest in both firearms and self-defense courses as well as thousands of civilians from all walks of life through his company Top Firearms Instruction. He has created law enforcement training programs as well as community programs for gun safety and bully prevention for children. Tyson is a certified instructor for the world famous Gracie University and a Master Instructor for the Carotid Restraint Institute and Compliant Technologies. He has successfully competed in several shooting matches over the last decade, and served as range safety officer and match director for several shooting competitions across the Midwest. Tyson has written several magazine articles that have appeared in international online publications such as PoliceOne, CorrectionsOne, American Shooting Journal, and Brazilian Jiu Jitsu Eastern Europe.

Made in the USA
Columbia, SC
16 February 2020